DECOLONIZING DEMOCRACY

DECOLONIZING DEMOCRACY

TRANSFORMING THE SOCIAL CONTRACT IN INDIA

CHRISTINE KEATING

THE PENNSYLVANIA STATE UNIVERSITY PRESS
UNIVERSITY PARK, PENNSYLVANIA

Chapter 3, "Framing the Postcolonial Social Contract," first appeared in a different version in *Hypatia: A Journal of Feminist Philosophy* 22, no. 4 (Fall 2007).

Library of Congress Cataloging-in-Publication Data

Keating, Christine.
Decolonizing democracy : transforming the social contract in India / Christine Keating.
p. cm.
Includes bibliographical references and index.
Summary: "Analyzes the movement for Indian independence, the framing of the Indian Constitution, and contemporary contestations over women's legal and political status as crucial moments of transition in which feminist and other progressive activists in India have challenged racialized and gendered underpinnings of democracy's social contract"—Provided by publisher.
ISBN 978-0-271-04863-5 (cloth : alk. paper)
1. Women's rights—India.
2. Women—Legal status, laws, etc.—India.
3. Feminism—India.
4. Constitutional history—India.
5. Social contract.
I. Title.

HQ1236.5.I4K43   2011
305.420954—dc22
2011003135

It is the policy of The Pennsylvania State University Press to use acid-free paper. Publications on uncoated stock satisfy the minimum requirements of American National Standard for Information Sciences—Permanence of Paper for Printed Library Material, ANSI Z39.48–1992.

The Pennsylvania State University Press is a member of the Association of American University Presses.

This book is printed on Natures Natural, which contains 50% post-consumer waste.

CONTENTS

ACKNOWLEDGMENTS

This book could not have been written without the intellectual and political companionship and support of many people.

I was very lucky to have been a part of three exciting political projects while I was writing this book, projects that have given me both a deep sense of hope in the possibility of political, social, and economic change and the opportunity to experience the joy of being a part of such change. First, I would like to thank my fellow collective members, past and present, of La Escuela Popular Norteña, a popular education collective geared to building coalitions against multiple oppressions, which for the last twenty years has profoundly shaped my political vision and practice. Special thanks to María Lugones, whose politically engaged teaching and scholarship sparked my passion for feminist and antiracist organizing and political work.

I was also very glad to be in the right place at the right time at the University of Washington as the struggle for TA unionization reached its apex. Thanks to my fellow members of the GSEAC organizing committee—the late night meetings and phone-banking sessions as well as early mornings on the picket line resulted not only in collective bargaining rights for graduate student employees at the University of Washington, but also in enduring friendships.

Thanks as well to fellow members of the QIV-C community in New York, who challenged and inspired me and my family with their commitment to live with clear intention and integrity. Their example of collective, non-hierarchical decision-making on matters both large and small demonstrates both the possibility and the value of creating alternative social structures in our present.

This book benefited from the encouragement and critical feedback from a number of mentors, colleagues, and friends including Asma Abbas, S. M. Amadae, Roni Amit, Rochana Bajpai, Franco Barchiesi, Tom Beer, Amy Bonomi, Carlo Bonura, Cindy Burack, Susan Burgess, Jill Bystydzienski,

Luis Cabrera, Aimee Carrillo Rowe, Varsha Chitnis, Mat Coleman, Fred Dallmayr, Laila Farah, Jane Flax, Kaushik Ghosh, Carol Gould, Amy Hamilton, Astrid Henry, Nancy Hirschmann, Valerie Hunt, Lynn Itagaki, Deema Kaedbey, Vera Eccarius Kelly, Laura DuMond Kerr, Ken Lang, Kristin Larson, Guisela LaTorre, Sheena Malhotra, Kimberly Manning, Charles Mills, Linda Mizejewski, Tamir Moustafa, Isis Nusair, Carole Pateman, Kimberlee Perez, Venkat Rao, András Rátonyi, Natasha Rosenblatt, Shireen Roshanravan, Francesca Royster, Ann Russo, Ki-young Shin, Wendy Smooth, Wendy Somerson, Mytheli Sreenivas, Mary Thomas, Pamela Trivedi, Rebecca Wanzo, Meredith Weiss, and Judy Tzu-Chun Wu. I am particularly grateful to Christine Di Stefano, Nancy Hartsock, Priti Ramamurthy, Paul Brass, Frank Conlon, and Mary Callahan for their invaluable support and mentorship in shaping this project in its early stages. Thanks as well to all my colleagues and students at the University of Washington, Saint Mary's College, Siena College, and the Ohio State University who made those institutions great places to work and to teach. The academic life can be a bit of an itinerant one; thanks to my dear friends in Seattle, South Bend, New York, and Ohio for making all those places feel like home. Thanks also to the feminist political theory group at the Western Political Science Association meetings, which has been an invaluable source of camaraderie and intellectual reinvigoration. Sandy Thatcher, Kendra Boileau, Suzanne Wolk, and all of the editorial staff at Penn State Press have been wonderful, and I very much appreciate their guidance and input.

Much of the research for this book was done at the Nehru Memorial Museum and Library in New Delhi and the University of Washington Library in Seattle; I am grateful to the very helpful staff at both of those institutions and for the depth and richness of their collections. Many thanks to the Gupta family in New Delhi whose loving care, early morning yoga sessions, and late-night conversations made my research stay in India particularly delightful. Special thanks goes to Melissa Meade, on whose porches I wrote much of this book. Our summer writing camps combined thought-provoking conversation, reading, writing, neighborhood strolling, and evening card playing in fun and always inspiring ways.

Throughout the project, Larin McLaughin lovingly endured the ups and downs of the writing process with me. The years I spent writing this book were much better for her companionship, keen mind, and editorial prowess, not to mention her sunshine smile. To her, and to our children, Maddie and Gabriel, I am deeply grateful. Maddie drew a beautiful picture of our family for the cover for the book. Much to her chagrin, the press decided to go with another cover idea, but her picture will always remind me of how much this book was a family project. Many thanks as well to McLaughlin family for offering diversions and adventures, especially for the kids, during the long gestation of this project. I would also like to extend my deep appreciation to the Perera-Richardson-Jafferjee family in Sri Lanka, especially Saku, Anu, Ranjini (Hamu), Maurice (Pops), Chris and Fallon, who have welcomed me into their song and laughter-filled homes in Sri Lanka for so many years now and always have made me feel like a beloved member of the family. Last but definitely not least, I would like to thank my wonderful family of origin—many thanks and much love to Ted, Emily, Olivia and Christopher Keating; Peter, Alice, Natalie, and Sarah Keating; Bill Keating; Joe Keating; Cathy and Ben Miller; Meredith Hahn; Cheryl Conway and Melany Burrill; Chris, Kevan, Brennan, and Tucker Full; Bill, Diane, Craig, and Sari Conway; and the dear memories of Helen and Bill Conway, my grandparents. To my parents, Susan Keating and Sonny Hersch: words cannot express my gratitude for their love, encouragement, wise counsel, and unflagging enthusiasm for this project along every step of the way.

Introduction: Decolonizing Democracy

December 9, 1946, was an extraordinary day in the history of democracy. On that day, Indian delegates to the Constituent Assembly, the body convened to frame a new constitution for an India free from British colonial rule, met for the first time. The task before the Constituent Assembly, as the future prime minister Jawaharlal Nehru declared in his opening speech, was the forging of a new, more egalitarian model of democracy, what he called the "fullest democracy," which would abolish discrimination on the basis of religion, race, caste, and sex.[1] Despite this pledge, however, the Assembly produced a deeply ambiguous constitution that perpetuated the legal subordination of women and the political marginalization of both women and minority groups, even while it asserted gender, racial, caste, and religious equality as a fundamental right.

Why, when the framers were intent on building an inclusive, egalitarian democracy, did they produce a constitution that so compromised justice for women and minority groups? In this book, I argue that this contradictory outcome is in part linked to what could be called a politics of compensatory domination in which political authorities seek to build consent to their rule by consolidating and/or enabling forms of intergroup and intragroup rule. The central normative argument of this book is that the ongoing project of making our political relations more democratic requires challenging this politics of compensatory domination.

In making this argument, I analyze the reconfiguration of what Carole Pateman and Charles Mills call, respectively, the sexual and racial contracts underpinning liberal democratic theory in the transition to independence in India. I suggest that the racialized fraternal democratic order Pateman and Mills describe was significantly challenged by the nationalist and feminist struggles against British colonialism in India but was reshaped into what I call a postcolonial social contract by the framers of the new Indian constitution. I explore contemporary struggles that link movements for gender and minority group justice in ways that challenge the contradictions embedded in the contract and point the way to more just configurations of democratic solidarity.

APPROACH: CRITICAL CONTRACT THEORY

As an approach to understanding political life, social contract theory focuses on the terms and conditions of consent to political authority. Social contract theorists address a central question: Why, if we are all free and equal, would a person accept being ruled by others? The urgency of this question arose in part when political and social upheavals debunked distinctions such as noble birth, the divine right of kings, or the natural rule of the father as adequate justification for political authority. Instead, political theorists such as Thomas Hobbes, in *The Leviathan,* and John Locke, in his *Second Treatise of Government,* argued that legitimate political authority is grounded in an agreement among equals—a social contract—in which citizens consent to exchange their natural freedom for the order and protection a government supposedly can provide.

This project is written in the methodological vein of what might be called critical social contract theory, a subset of social contract theory. While Hobbes and Locke suggest that it is in our best interests to submit to political authority, theorists more critical of such an agreement use a social contract approach to point to less benign reasons why supposedly free and equal people might agree to obey the state. For example, Jean-Jacques Rousseau, in *Discourse on the Origin of Inequality,* Carole Pateman in *The Sexual Contract,* and Charles Mills in *The Racial Contract* retell contract stories in order to uncover the operative power relations in the polity and the values that justify them. Instead of seeking to legitimate political authority, these critical social contract theorists ask the following kinds of questions: What are the terms and conditions of the social contract? What groups are included or excluded as signatories of such a contract? Does the social contract benefit some groups over others? These questions help to elucidate, in the words of Charles Mills, the "non-ideal contract at the heart of the ideal contract."[2] According to Rousseau, for example, the social contract generates a political order that protects the property of the rich. In contemporary political theory, Pateman and Mills argue that the often hidden motivations for the transference of political sovereignty from self to state include the consolidation of gender and racial power. For Pateman and Mills, respectively, the social contract is both a sexual and a racial contract.

In Pateman's framing, a sexual contract that organizes men's exploitive access to women's sexuality and labor underlies the social contract. For Pateman, although the social contract disrupted the paternal patriarchal rule of the father in Western political theory by holding that all men should be considered equal, it reaffirmed the rule of the sons—the brothers—over women and thus heralded a new, specifically fraternal patriarchal order. In *The Racial Contract*, Charles Mills underscores the limited membership of this fraternity—it is restricted to whites. He asserts that the social contract is not only a sexual but also a racial contract in that it "establishes a racial polity, a racial state, and a racial juridical system, where the status of whites and non-whites is clearly demarcated, whether by law or custom."[3]

Social contract theorists have used a variety of narrative devices to make their arguments. These often involve telling social contract stories, stories that describe an agreement that establishes the terms and conditions of political association in a polity. These can be real events or they can be conjectural.[4] Hobbes, Locke, and Rousseau, for example, all ask us to imagine a state of nature out of which people agree to come together in political community. In his influential book *A Theory of Justice*, John Rawls describes a hypothetical situation in which participants are ignorant of their particularities as they seek to agree on terms of justice that will link them in their political solidarity. In *The Sexual Contract*, Carole Pateman analyzes the work of political theorists in her narrative of the origins of a sexual contract in Western liberal political thought. Charles Mills takes a different approach in *The Racial Contract* and combines both theoretical and historical analysis to trace the development of a racial contract. The social contract story told in this book has its roots in historical and contemporary events and is drawn from primary and secondary accounts of these events, with a particular focus on the proceedings of the Constituent Assembly and parliamentary debates in India. In using documents such as these to tell the story of the postcolonial social contract, I follow the example of Jane Flax, who, in *The American Dream in Black and White*, analyzes the transcripts of the Clarence Thomas Senate confirmation hearings in order to examine the interplay of race and gender in American democracy. Flax argues that these hearings should be understood as "political dramas" whose "characters, story lines, and dialogue, both overt and covert," illuminate the tremendous amount of work involved in maintaining the racial and sexual contracts that underlie U.S. democracy.[5] My own approach traces historical events in India such as the consolidation of British colonial rule, the struggle for independence, the framing of the new constitution, and contemporary debates over women's legal and political status as crucial scenes in a social contract drama in which the actors negotiate and rewrite the terms and conditions of democratic governance.

The stories embedded within social contract theory are not meant to be either literal or fictional—indeed, Pateman refers to them as "conjectural histories"—instead, the stories provide a conceptual framework for understanding political relations.[6] Charles Mills explains that the contract "provides an iconography, a set of images, that is immensely powerful and appealing, in large measure because it makes most salient, in simplified and abstract form, the modern idea of society and all its various institutions and practices (the state, the legal system) as human creations. . . . [It provides,] at the basic level of a conceptual framework, a picture, a story, an overarching optic for thinking about the socio-political."[7] In my own argument, for example, I do not hold that the Indian Constituent Assembly convened in order to draw up a postcolonial social contract, but I do suggest that the postcolonial social contract is "real" in that it structures political and social relations among people. In writing conjectural histories, critical contract theory shares with a genealogical approach an interest in generating what Michel Foucault calls "counter-memories."[8] Whereas genealogy distances itself from a search for origins, however, critical contract theory constructs origin stories in order to elucidate power relations.

Taking inspiration from the insights of feminists like Kimberlé Crenshaw, who emphasizes that processes of race and gender (and of group subordination in general) cannot be understood in isolation from one another, as well as from Pateman and Mills themselves, who argue that the racial and sexual contracts must be considered together,[9] this study analyzes the close links between the racial and sexual contracts in a postcolonial context. This project thus highlights ways in which relations of intra- and inter-group subordination often constitute or buttress political authority.

As important as the ways in which racial and sexual contracts function together are the ways in which people resist the power inequities engendered by these intersecting sexual and racial contracts. Critical contract theory has been very useful in elucidating how concepts such as "freedom" and "equality" have been compatible with subordination in democratic polities. The emphasis on exposing the deep-rooted nature of racism and sexism in democratic theory and practice, however, has generally come at the expense of attention to questions of resistance. Although both Pateman and Mills acknowledge the presence—and thus the possibility—of resistance, they do not substantially address oppositional practices and movements and their effects on the contracts in their theories; the contracts, as Nancy Fraser observed in her review of *The Sexual Contract*, thus seem "impervious to resistance and change."[10] By analyzing the reworking of democracy's racial and sexual contracts in Indian independence, this study centers on questions of resistance by asking the following questions: In what ways did challenges to the racial contract in the struggle against colonialism in India engender challenges to the sexual contract, and vice versa? How did the Constituent Assembly consolidate or compromise these challenges to the racial and sexual contracts in the new postcolonial democracy they forged? How are the struggles against gender, caste, and minority group subordination linked in contemporary politics? Exploring these questions can point to ways in which the racial and sexual contracts are open to challenge and contestation.

By reconfiguring the racialized and gendered terms and conditions of rule, the postcolonial social contract that emerged during the transition to independence in India can be thought of as both a postcolonial racial contract and a postcolonial sexual contract. Whereas the sexual and racial contracts that Pateman and Mills describe are primarily domination contracts, the postcolonial racial and sexual contracts are both liberation and domination contracts. On the one hand, for example, the very act of writing the Indian constitution in 1946 constituted a radical rejection of the racialized logic of colonial rule, which held that Indians were not "ready" for democratic self-rule. Further marking the postcolonial racial contract in India as a liberation contract, the Indian constitution expressly forbids discrimination on the basis of race, religion, or caste. On the other hand, however, the framers consolidated Hindu political hegemony by rejecting measures that would have ensured adequate political representation for minority groups, in particular for Muslims, thus reinscribing the racial contract as, in part, a domination contract. The postcolonial sexual contract embedded in the Indian postcolonial social contract has similarly contradictory impulses. On the one hand, it is liberating, in that it removes formal restrictions to public political life for women and enshrines equality on the basis of sex as a fundamental right. On the other hand, it functions as a domination contract in that it affirms and consolidates women's legal subordination in the areas of property ownership, inheritance, marriage, and divorce.

In contrast to the ways that sexual and racial contracts submerge the contradiction between democracy's ethos of equality and the reality of gender and racial subordination, the clauses in the Indian constitution that assert gender, race, religious, and caste equality leave these contradictions exposed and thus open to challenge by subordinate groups pressing for justice. I explore such challenges in this book and suggest that they point the way toward an expressively egalitarian reformulation of the social contract that enables and fosters the participatory construction of social and political solidarity.

COMPENSATORY DOMINATION

In *Contract and Domination*, Pateman notes that "the point of the social contract is that in the modern state individuals give up their right of self-government to another or a few others."[11] In her earlier work, Pateman notes that the paradigmatic agreement in social contract theory is quite particular (and peculiar): it is a promise to obey. One of the strengths of radical or critical contract theory is that it helps to explain why people in positions of power and privilege along lines of class, gender, and race might agree to be ruled by others—it is in their interest to do so insofar as the state backs up that power and privilege. But why would those who lack such advantages submit to that rule? For Pateman and Mills, women and people of color, respectively, do *not* agree to be ruled, because they are in fact excluded from the contract—they are subject to it but not subjects of it. The submission of subordinate groups to the terms and conditions of exclusionary contracts is achieved by force and by ideological conditioning, not by free consent. Rousseau points to an additional possibility—that marginalized groups (the poor and propertyless) acquiesce in the authority of a law that shackles their freedom because "looking more below them than above them, domination becomes more dear to them than independence, and they consent to wear chains in order to be able to give them in turn to others."[12] In Rousseau's view, in other words, subordinate groups allow themselves to be ruled by those above them so as to rule those below them (whether in the present or in the future hope of such rule).[13]

While Rousseau's formulation is helpful in directing attention to substate relations of rule, its explanatory power rests in part on the implicit assumption that the desire to dominate is inherent in human beings and that the ruling classes can "trick" the poor into submitting to class rule by exploiting this desire. I argue, by contrast, that the impulse to rule is constructed and that state actors often use ideological conditioning (and sometimes force) to pressure or entice dominant members of a structurally subordinate group to exercise command as part of the process of manufacturing consent, or at least of establishing acquiescence. In colonial India, for example, where customs and practices related to gender were extremely heterogeneous and plural—some more egalitarian than others—the British actively shaped and imposed as law particularly inegalitarian gender relations. The British could thus present the racial contract as a fraternal bargain: what colonized men lost in political power they could regain in masculinist control over the family. Note, however, that this is not by any means a "natural" or "traditional" form of control but rather one that was coercively imposed. In this configuration of racial rule, gains in masculinist power compensated (however inadequately) for loss of political power along ethnic and racial lines. I call this the politics of "compensatory domination."

I would suggest that in addition to ideology and force, compensatory domination is a third component that promotes submission to inequitable social contracts. According to James Scott, we have to differentiate between settings in which a thick version of hegemony (grounded in consent) might obtain and those in which a thin version, or even, in his words, a "paper-thin" version, of hegemony (grounded in resignation or resignation only under certain conditions) might obtain.[14] I argue that the logic of compensatory domination acts as a "thickening agent" for conservative social and political formations by generating investments in hegemonic configurations of rule.

The notion of compensatory domination provides three linked lines of inquiry to pursue toward the goal of challenging inequitable forms of rule. The first focuses on the state: In what ways have state actors supported or consolidated relations of domination within and between groups in order to secure the state's authority? The second line of inquiry is closely related to the first but focuses on subordinated groups' own stakes in a social contract that sets the terms and conditions for their own marginalization or oppression: In what ways have oppressed groups allowed themselves to be ruled in exchange for ruling over others? The third line of inquiry focuses on the possibilities of resistance: In what ways have challenges to compensatory domination destabilized inequitable relations of rule?

While the concept of compensatory domination implies complicity on the part of subordinate groups in their own domination (albeit highly coerced complicity), it also suggests the possibility of resistance (albeit highly constrained): If one has consented to inequitable rule, one can refuse that rule as well. Indeed, as a corollary to his assertion that people agree to be ruled in order to rule others, Rousseau notes that "it is very difficult to reduce to obedience someone who does not seek to command."[15] As I show in this book, the struggle for Indian independence is one illustration of the tremendous power of collective refusal of the politics of compensatory domination; as we shall see, the nationalist and feminist refusal of masculinist control over women played an important role in the success of the struggle against British colonialism.

LEARNING FROM INDIAN POLITICS

This book looks at India from the early eighteenth century to the present, analyzing through the lens of critical contract theory the politics of colonialism, nationalism, and contemporary struggles for gender, caste, and communal justice. It makes sense, for several reasons, to focus on India in a study of postcolonial democracy and the reconfiguration of the racial and sexual contracts. First, the successful movement against colonial rule in India—a direct challenge to the racial contract that held that people of color were not fit for self-rule—has inspired and continues to inspire liberation struggles across the globe. Second, in addition to being the largest democracy in the world, India is also one of the most complex and diverse democracies in the world, with a polity that is structured, often hierarchically, along gender, caste,[16] class, religious/communal,[17] and tribal lines.[18] Finally, India has extremely vigorous and vital movements for social justice that continue to challenge and rework both the meaning and practice of democracy in innovative and potentially more just ways.

The study of Indian politics can extend and develop critical contract theory. First, it contributes to our understanding of the colonial contract as an important subset of the racial contract. Charles Mills writes that the racial contract is made up of three "subcontracts": the expropriation contract, the slave contract, and the colonial contract. It is the colonial contract, Mills argues, that legitimated European "rule over the nations in Asia, Africa, and the Pacific" and that established the modern world as a "racial polity."[19] Rather than justify colonial expansion by force, status, or divine right, European colonists justified their rule by positing the tacit agreement of the colonized. Of course, the notion that colonial rule was based on the free agreement of the colonized was a fiction, and the colonial contract, like the other racial subcontracts, had to be enforced though violence, ideological conditioning, and, as this study suggests, compensatory domination. In this book I explore the shifting justificatory logic and enabling collaborations on which colonial projections of "consent" depended.

In telling the story of the postcolonial social contract in India, this book extends the critical contract tradition by paying close attention to the ways in which actors in postcolonial democratic contexts deploy and negotiate various iterations of the social contract, and thus contributes to the field of comparative political theory. While scholars of political theory in the United States and Europe have focused predominantly on Western political thought, members of a growing subgroup in the discipline assert the importance of comparative political theory. One of the strengths of comparative political theory as a subfield is its challenge to institutional structures and modes of theorizing that exclude or marginalize non-Western political thought. In *Unthinking Eurocentrism*, Ella Shohat and Robert Stam write that Eurocentrism elides non-European political traditions while at the same time it masks the West's role in subverting those traditions, particularly democratic ones. Eurocentric theories that suppress, or at the very least fail to stimulate curiosity about, democratic innovation in non-Western contexts are not only congruent with neocolonial interventions abroad in the name of democracy; they also impoverish the political imaginations of those in the West by neglecting the exciting and transformative work that is recasting democracy in more egalitarian and inclusive terms in postcolonial polities. For example, Rajeev Bhargava notes that "for all talk of the fact of pluralism and multiculturalism, the mention of how such issues arise or are tackled in India is astoundingly infrequent. . . . Debates around the world on issues such as group rights, secession, differentiated citizenship, affirmative action, and gender-equality are bound to be considerably enriched by the Indian experience."[20] Given that social contract is in many respects the lingua franca of political theory, interpreting Indian political innovations through the lens of social contract enables the translation of these developments across contexts. By highlighting Indian independence as a significant moment of transition in which nationalists and feminists challenged and reworked the racial and sexual contracts upon which liberal democratic theory rests, I am arguing for the centrality of the Indian political tradition in the history of democratic theory. The study of India's successes and setbacks in establishing the Constituent Assembly's proclaimed goal of building an inclusive and egalitarian democracy promotes a fuller understanding of democracy's history and future possibilities.

In addition to extending the critical contract approach, this study makes several contributions to understanding gendered colonial and postcolonial politics in India. First, it unpacks two distinct but interrelated approaches to colonial governance: colonial paternalism and colonial fraternalism. In the colonial paternalist framing of colonial rule, control over women is justificatory: The supposed illegitimate exercise of masculinist power by Indian men over Indian women is considered justification for colonial intervention, what Gayatri Chakravorty Spivak refers to as the colonial rhetoric of "white men saving brown women from brown men."[21] In contrast, the colonial fraternalist approach to colonial rule seeks to foster close alliances with elite men and to pursue policies that were either "hands off" with respect to gender relations or tended to enhance masculinist control over women (e.g., the restrictions placed upon women's ability to own property). While scholars have focused primarily on the colonial paternalist approach, I suggest that the fraternalist approach also played a crucially important role in the consolidation of colonial rule.

Second, attention to the politics of compensatory domination helps to flesh out an understanding of the various components of resistance to colonial rule. The story of how the nationalist movement disarmed the relations of force that underlie colonial rule through nonviolent resistance is well known. So, too, is the story of how the nationalist movement discredited the colonial ideology that Indians were not ready for self-rule. The story of how the nationalist movement worked with the feminist movement to challenge relations of compensatory domination, however, is less well known. In this book, I highlight resistance to the gendered and racialized logic of both colonial paternalism and colonial fraternalism as an important component of the anticolonial struggle, in that it undercut both the justificatory rhetoric and the enabling alliances upon which British rule depended.

This argument about the centrality of gender resistance to British rule expands on Partha Chatterjee's influential reading of the relationship between nationalism and the "woman question" in India in *The Nation and Its Fragments*. Chatterjee notes that in the mid-nineteenth century nationalists refused to debate the "woman question" with the British after decades of acrimony over the question. He argues that this refusal was an important component of resistance to imperial rule, because "to allow the intimate domain of the family to become amenable to the discursive regulations of the political domain [would have] meant a surrender of autonomy."[22] I argue that the nationalist approach did not end simply in the reassertion of indigenous masculinist control over women. Instead, challenging British rule also involved resisting the inequitable gender relations that the British fostered during their rule. I trace the emergence of what could be called a "resistant convergence" of the women's and nationalist movements in the anticolonial struggle, a convergence marked by overlapping leadership and participation in each other's campaigns. Working together for women's suffrage and the reform of personal law, Indian feminist and nationalist groups in the early twentieth century exposed the hollowness of British paternalist claims that they were protectors of Indian womanhood and refused fraternalist control over women as compensation for continued colonial rule.[23] Together, these groups destabilized—if only briefly—the logic of compensatory domination so central to colonial rule.

Howard Winant has argued that the end of World War II heralded a "worldwide rupture of the racial status quo," a momentous break with patterns of worldwide racial domination that marked the modern world so deeply. He explains that movements against colonization and antiracist and civil rights struggles combined "to problematize the forms of rule and cultural norms for states and social systems where hegemony was organized (as it almost universally was) along racial lines." Taking different forms in different places, these movements won reforms ranging from "decolonization to belated enfranchisement and the granting of formal citizenship rights." Winant notes, however, that the rupture of the racial status quo, though decisive, was not conclusive and that patterns of racial inequality, hierarchy, and domination not only survived but "adapted and modernized to post-colonial conditions." One aspect of this adaptation, he suggests, is that race, both as a concept and as a practice, has become diffused and transformed, such that a variety of differences are undergoing what he calls a "racialized articulation," even in places, such as South Asia and East Asia, that are often thought of as free from racial conflict.[24] For example, Zaheer Baber argues that in India "communal identities have been 'racialized' and recurring conflicts share striking structural and ideological similarities with racial conflicts in other parts of the world." Baber suggests that particularly with respect to the relationship between Hindus and Muslims in India, there is "racism without race." "Provided one accepts the idea that racial differences are not directly derived from phenotypical characteristics but are indeed socially constructed," he writes, "one can see that the logic at work in India is similar to the logic of racial conflict, with its attendant conflicts over resources, residential segregation, violently enforced endogamy, armory of stereotypes, myth-making and invented histories."[25] Focusing on the racial dimension of the postcolonial social contract highlights the transformation of colonial racial hierarchy—the dramatic rupture of democracy's "color line" in independent India—to a more complex rearticulation of racialized rule, one that mandates racial, communal/religious, and caste equality yet nonetheless structures hierarchies within and between these groups.

DECOLONIZATION AND DEMOCRACY

This study aims to both document and contribute to the long and ongoing struggle to reclaim democracy on behalf of struggles for decolonization when both colonial and neocolonial interventions are so often made in its name. In the introduction to their influential collection *Feminist Genealogies, Colonial Legacies, Democratic Futures*, M. Jacqui Alexander and Chandra Talpade Mohanty suggest the need for "a working definition of feminist democracy which is anti-capitalist and centered on the project of decolonization."[26] This book takes up Alexander and Mohanty's challenge to move toward a decolonial feminist democratic politics by focusing on the colonial history of the relationship between authority and consent in democratic theory and practice and its links to inter- and intragroup subordination. I suggest that the project of reclaiming democracy on behalf of decolonization struggles involves a critical examination of the ways in which the terms and conditions of democracy itself have been articulated in relation to the politics of compensatory domination—a politics that is deeply implicated in the history of colonial rule worldwide—such that what we understand and practice as democracy needs to be subjected to a process of decolonization. In Alexander and Mohanty's terms, decolonization involves the everyday processes of making "sense of the world in relationship to hegemonic power" and of "engagement with democratic collectivities which are premised on the ideas of autonomy and self determination."[27] In terms of the process of decolonizing democracy, I argue that a critical task involves an analysis of how democratic concepts and practices have been shaped in relation to the politics of compensatory domination; an interrogation of one's own and others' insertion in practices that are interwoven in the politics of compensatory domination; an exploration of alternative modes of democratic solidarity, some of which may need to be recovered, some of which are still being practiced and may need to be amplified more widely, and some of which may need to be developed; and, finally, the everyday work of enacting those alternatives.

From a decolonial feminist perspective, the ways in which control over women became a term of exchange in the process of consolidating colonial rule in India, and the challenge to that strategy in the anticolonial struggle, are particularly significant. Understanding this process and this challenge is important not only for historical analyses but also for contemporary political struggles, given that the politics of compensatory domination as a means of gaining the consent obstinately echoes colonial relations of rule in present-day democratic politics. Indeed, although this book focuses on Indian politics, a postcolonial social contract that guarantees equality to women and minority groups, on the one hand, while instituting measures that legally subordinate and marginalize women and minority groups, on the other, is applicable to other contexts as well. Close consideration of the ways in which sexual and racial contracts were contested and reconfigured in the transition to independence in India can help us understand the interplay of gender and minority rights in multicultural democracies more generally. The 1996 South African constitution, for example, one of the most progressive democratic constitutions in the world, simultaneously asserts gender equality as a fundamental right and recognizes customary laws, many of which discriminate deeply against women. The 2005 Iraqi constitution enshrines gender equality and facilitates women's participation in politics (for example, it mandates that 25 percent of seats in the legislature be filled by women), but it also establishes Iraqis' right to be "free in their personal status according to their religions, sects, beliefs, or choices," which in practice translates into heavy discrimination against women. In both cases, the relationship between the equality clause and the discriminatory customary laws is ambiguous, leaving open to negotiation the question of how to resolve the tension between them. Study of the ways in which consent to inequitable relations of rule in both the colonial and postcolonial contexts has been enabled by intra- or intergroup domination reveals the tragic cost of investments in such so-called privileges, as oppressed groups become complicit in their own subordination. Such attention can, I suggest, be an important part of the process of what Spivak calls "unlearning one's privilege as loss."[28]

While examining the politics of compensatory domination is the central analytic work of this book, exploring alternative modes of egalitarian political solidarity is its primary normative goal. To this end, struggles against subordination on the basis of gender, caste, and minority status in India suggest possibilities for challenging the politics of compensatory domination on the subjective, group, and state levels. In thinking about how to apply the lessons of India more widely, I draw on the examples of these struggles to call for a politics geared to building and fostering egalitarian relations within often highly constrained settings.

ON DOMINATION AND RESISTANCE

In its focus on relationships of domination and resistance, this book pays particular attention to the power relations among and within groups. By "group" I mean a social collectivity that is marked or in some way designated as distinct, whether that marking is imposed from without or articulated internally, on the basis of race, gender, caste, class, religion, among other characteristics. Although I am interested in all of these criteria for group membership, this study focuses on processes of racial and gender differentiation and stratification that were challenged and reconfigured in the transition to independence in India and mapped onto identity formations such as those based on caste, religion, and ethnicity in postcolonial India.

I understand gender and race as constructed social categories that have been invented and elaborated in order to serve power but can also serve as potential sources of solidarity and resistance. Following the work of María Lugones, Uma Chakravarti, Kimberlé Crenshaw, Nivedita Menon, and others, I look at the ways in which the interplay of multiple lines of oppression differentiate and stratify these groupings internally. Lugones, for example, argues that colonialism "imposed a new gender system that created very different arrangements for colonized males and females than for white bourgeois colonizers."[29] I suggest that differentiation and internal stratification within a social group can serve as a source of cooptation and acquiescence—a white bourgeois colonizing woman, for example, might submit to relations of subordination because she is invested in the dominance that her membership in the white bourgeois class allows her to exercise over the colonized. At the same time, however, such differentiation and internal stratification can illuminate the contradictions inherent in the politics of compensatory domination by underscoring the links between one's own and another's subordination.

Several assumptions about our place in relations of domination and subordination and our ability to maneuver and resist these relations support the analysis that follows. First, I assume that most of us are located in positions that enforce both our dominance (that is, we are enticed or compelled to set rules that others must follow) and our subordination (that is, we are enticed or compelled to obey rules that others have set) within a complex set of social, economic, and political relations. Next, I emphasize that the desire to dominate others is not self-generating; there is nothing inherent in human nature that drives us to dominate. Rather, I assume that dominance has both rewards and costs and that those who are powerful in some ways (but structurally subordinate in others) are often subjected to enormous pressure to engage in dominating others. I am particularly interesting in investigating how oppressed groups are enticed or pressured to dominate others, whether within their group or outside it, for the purpose of consolidating the power and authority of the state.

Fundamental to this project is the idea that we are not passive in relation to the structures of power that we are inserted into and that both dominant and subordinate positionings can be resisted or refused. In making this assumption, I follow the work of James Scott and others who have argued for attention to a variety of forms of resistance to domination, resistances that may be small or large, organized or spontaneous, easily understood as resistance or obscured by readings of them as trivial (or criminal), public or very circumspect.[30]

Finally, I assume that specific forms of domination and subordination are deeply contingent on one another. According to Elsa Barkley Brown, in order to build effective and inclusive feminist coalitions, "we need to recognize not only differences but also the relational nature of those differences. . . . White women and women of color not only live different lives but white women live the lives they do in large part because women of color live the ones they do."[31] In Brown's account, building feminist solidarity requires critical reflection on one's own insertion into structures of power. For her, women are closely linked across difference, but not innocently so. Our "unity" lies in the fact that we are all connected because of our relational insertion into hierarchies of domination and subordination, hierarchies that we also can resist and transform. It is toward such transformations that this book is geared.

OVERVIEW OF THE BOOK

Chapter 1 analyzes the shifting discourses of race and gender in British colonial rule in India. Recent works on the justificatory strategies of colonial rule in India have focused primarily on the logic of paternalism and its linked tropes of "saving" women in the empire and of racial and cultural difference. I argue that it is important to pay close attention to fraternalism as a justificatory strategy of colonial rule as well. The fraternalist approach to colonial rule emphasized a racial kinship between the colonizers and the colonized elite and was characterized by policies that consolidated control over women in the family. I examine both paternalism and fraternalism as components of a larger politics of compensatory domination in which consent to colonial authority was engendered by countenancing, structuring, and enabling forms of inter- and intragroup rule.

Chapter 2 looks at the "resistant convergence" of the women's and nationalist movements in the struggle to end colonial rule in India. I argue that the relationship between these movements, though often fraught and uneven, was marked by overlapping leadership and by the participation of people in both movements in critical, mutually reinforcing ways. Through an analysis of the campaigns for women's suffrage in India in the early twentieth century, I suggest that these movements rejected the logic of both colonial paternalism and colonial fraternalism and effectively challenged the politics of compensatory domination. This chapter argues that women's and nationalist groups thus challenged colonial authority in part by destabilizing the equation of control over women with cultural autonomy that was central to both the fraternal and the paternal approaches to colonial rule in India.

Chapter 3 focuses on the Constituent Assembly's framing of the new Indian constitution (1946–50). I examine the challenges and opportunities the framers faced in their goal of forging a model of democracy that would abolish discrimination on the basis of sex, race, religion, and caste. In building such a new democracy, I suggest, the framers struggled to reconcile their commitment to an egalitarian polity founded on caste, minority group, and gender equality with their efforts to generate consent for the political authority of the new government. I argue that the Assembly settled on a compromise to resolve this dilemma: they established equality in the public sphere as a fundamental right for women, low-caste groups, and minority groups, but at the same time consolidated the legal subordination of women in the family and the political marginalization of both women and religious minority groups in the new Indian polity. I see this compromise as a central component of a postcolonial social contract, a new form of the social contract that both advances and compromises gender, caste, and minority group rights.

Chapters 4 and 5 analyze challenges to the postcolonial social contract in contemporary Indian politics. In chapter 4, I examine the debate over the Women's Reservation Bill, a bill that would amend the constitution to provide for 33 percent representation for women in the Indian parliament. I look especially closely at the tensions between women's groups and underrepresented caste and minority groups on this issue, and I suggest that adding "subquotas" to the bill would productively link women's empowerment to lower-caste and minority group empowerment, thus challenging the politics of compensatory domination. In chapter 5, I direct attention to the fierce political controversies regarding personal law in present-day Indian politics. I distinguish between two forms of legal pluralism—fraternalist and egalitarian—and argue that the latter holds promise in linking struggles for minority group and gender rights.

Taking the lessons from struggles against women's legal subordination as a starting point, the Conclusion argues that the principles undergirding these efforts suggest possibilities for challenging the politics of compensatory domination on the intersubjective, group, and democratic-collective or state level. The Conclusion suggests possible directions for a politics geared to both the exploration and the enactment of alternative modes of democratic solidarity. In particular, it asserts that struggles against gender, caste, and minority group subordination and political marginalization in the Indian polity can point us toward a new social contract, what I call a "nondomination contract," an expressively egalitarian reformulation of the social contract that promotes the participatory construction of social and political solidarity.

1

Fraternalist and Paternalist Approaches to Colonial Rule

In *Liberalism and Empire,* Uday Mehta looks at the question of why liberal champions of freedom, equality, and consent within Europe supported, and sometimes even applauded, coercive rule in the colonies. To help explain the apparent paradox at work here, Mehta identifies a paternalist strain in liberal thought that allows for empire. Mehta observes that although it is an axiom of liberal theory that we are all born free and equal, liberal theorists such as John Locke and others also paternalistically assumed that we are not able to exercise that freedom or to participate in political community until we are adults. Mehta suggests that a racialization of the paternalist understanding of a developmental path toward citizenship justified imperialist coercion even in liberal thought: The colonized were seen as inhabiting an interme-diate stage between civilizational birth and adulthood and were assumed to be in need of political tutelage before they could become self-governing.[1]

Although Mehta does not focus on the gendered nature of colonial paternalism, postcolonial feminist scholars have emphasized the role that representations of women as victims or potential victims played in the elab-oration of paternalist justifications of colonial rule. For example, Gayatri Chakravorty Spivak, looking at the intersection of race, class, gender, and nation in the theory and practice of imperialism, writes that colonial dis-course about gender relations can be translated into the formula "We came, we saw, we were horrified, we intervened."[2] Such constructions of victim-ized womanhood in the colonies helped to elaborate a crucial notion of dif-ference between the colonizer and the colonized, because, as Anne Stoler asserts, referring to colonialism in Asia more generally, "colonial authority was constructed on . . . the notion that Europeans in the colonies made up an easily identifiable and discrete social entity."[3]

While paternalism and its linked tropes of "saving" women in the empire and of colonial racial difference are primary in much anticolonial analysis, we must also pay close attention to what I call a fraternalist approach to colonial rule. In many ways a fraternalist approach seems paternalism's opposite: It celebrates rather than disparages indigenous ways of being, emphasizes nonintervention rather than tutelage or assimilation, and works to consolidate rather than contest gender-based and other hierarchies. The interplay of fraternalism and paternalism in British colonial rhetoric and policy in India suggests, however, that although seemingly opposed in their approach to indigenous ways of life, these strategies reinforced each other and worked congruently—and often concurrently—to facilitate colonial rule in India.

This chapter focuses on the interplay of colonial paternalism and colonial fraternalism with respect to gender, caste, and communal or religious difference. On the one hand, the fraternalist approach to colonial rule relied on a discourse and politics of compensatory domination in which colonial administrators pursued policies that exacerbated or consolidated inter- and intragroup hierarchies to secure the acquiescence of elite groups in colonial rule. On the other hand, in the colonial paternalist framework, it was precisely these hierarchies, fostered and enabled by the colonial fraternalist approach but cast as traditional, that colonial administrators used to illustrate the necessity of colonial rule, in that the colonial state could supposedly manage community antagonisms and protect those in positions of subordination. Both approaches were deeply racialized and gendered, but differently so; whereas fraternalism emphasized civilizational or racial kinship and a shared masculinist bond between the colonized elite and the colonizers, colonial paternalism posited a stark racial difference between the colonizers and colonized and condemned indigenous masculinism.

BRITISH ORIENTALISTS AND THE POLITICS OF COLONIAL FRATERNALISM

In *The Sexual Contract*, Carole Pateman distinguishes between fraternal and paternal patriarchal accounts of political authority in Western political theory. In paternal patriarchal accounts, political authority is understood as analogous to the "natural" right of command that a father has over his children. Pateman argues that social contract theorists like Hobbes, Locke, and Rousseau rejected the political authority of the father in Western political theory and asserted the right of the sons—the brothers—to self-rule. In this account, the brothers—understood to be naturally free and equal—agree among themselves to establish political authority. Key to this agreement is a separation of "public" life from "private" life and a notion that some domains—such as family life—should be off limits to paternal authority. For Pateman, fraternalism, like paternalism before it, is deeply gendered: "Fraternity," she points out, "means what it says—the brotherhood of *men*."[4]

The notion of fraternalism—that is, a form of political authority grounded in a sense of brotherly unity or kinship, tacit consent, a separation of public and private spheres marked by nonintervention in family and religious life, and masculinist solidarity—is helpful for understanding the shifting and at times seemingly contradictory rhetoric used to justify colonial rule. Unlike the paternalist rejection of indigenous ways of being, the fraternalist approach emphasizes respect and admiration for indigenous philosophy and law to the extent that they are congruent with relations of colonial rule. Similarly, in contrast to paternalist discourses and policies that advocate intervention, the fraternalist approach advocates nonintervention in matters of religion and the family. Finally, like the rule of the brothers that Pateman describes, fraternalism as an approach to colonial rule both depends on and engenders masculinist solidarity.

In India, the colonial fraternalist approach was particularly pronounced in the early years of British rule and was associated with those scholar-administrators known as "Orientalists." In the late eighteenth century, the British East India Company went from being a mere trading entity in India to becoming a governing body with administrative and legislative control over Bengal and other provinces. The allegiance of elite groups within Bengal and the other provinces was key to the British East India Company's transition to administrative power in India. In his history of India, Burton Stein explains that "the first generation of colonial rulers could not have installed British authority but for the collaboration of powerful landed groups, wealthy commercial interests and influential scribes." This collaboration, he suggests, was in part obtained through judicial and land tenure policies that protected these elite groups' economic interests and persuaded them "to surrender their domination over minor administrative offices."[5] Indeed, as Nicholas Dirks explains, "colonialism was made possible, and then sustained and strengthened, as much by cultural technologies of rule as it was by the more obvious and brutal modes of conquest that first established power on foreign shores."[6] Scholar-administrators such as William Jones (1746–1794), a Supreme Court justice in India and the founder of the Asiatic Society in Bengal, and Warren Hastings (1732–1818), the first governor-general of India, were particularly influential in establishing the new governing framework for the British East India Company. Dubbed "Orientalists" for their intensive study of Oriental languages such as Sanskrit, these scholar-administrators shared an admiration for ancient Hindu literature, scripture, and law. At the heart of Orientalist rhetoric in India was the notion of a golden age of ancient Hindu civilization that was marked by prosperity, peace, and profound religious and philosophical insight. According to Orientalist historiography, this golden age was interrupted by Muslim invasions and long centuries of Muslim rule, during which Hindu civilization stagnated and declined. Rosanne Rocher explains that the British cast themselves in this story "as the protectors of a vast and suppliant majority that had been held under the thumb of Muslim oppressors."[7] In the Orientalist narrative, relations of colonial rule were established for the benefit of the Hindus, with the aim of reenfranchising them after years of Moghul rule.

A theory of civilizational and racial brotherhood between Hindus and the British animated the Orientalist account of the encounter between India and Britain. This theory was strengthened by William Jones's discovery of linguistic ties between Sanskrit and European languages, a link that for Orientalists pointed to the common ancestry of upper-caste Hindus and Europeans.[8] Early Orientalists like Jones celebrated this connection as further justification for the colonial project of recovering and translating ancient texts. Later Orientalists, in particular Max Muller, developed the notion of an "Aryan race" that included both the descendants of the Sanskrit-speaking population in India and Europeans, explaining that "Indians are one great branch of the Caucasian race . . . differing from other branches of the same race merely by its darker complexion caused by the climate." By casting the relationship between British and Hindus as one of racial kinship, Orientalists harnessed the language of racialized fraternity as a powerful tool of imperialist rhetoric. Muller, for example, exclaimed that "it is glorious to see [English] descendants of the same race . . . return to accomplish the work of civilization which had been left unfinished by their Aryan brethren."[9] In his study of the relationship between the concept of the Aryan race and British colonialism in India, Thomas Trautmann writes that it enabled the Orientalists to speak "of love and brotherhood as if colonial rule was a happy family reunion and coercion had nothing to do with it."[10]

The racialized fraternity imagined by the Orientalists was extremely circumscribed. For one thing, Orientalist narratives of a racial brotherhood and civilizational affinity between Hindu and British depended in part on depicting Muslims as racial others. Zaheer Baber notes that "British colonialism provided a major impetus for the dramatic consolidation of Hindu and Muslim identities. Aspects of Orientalist scholarship, focusing among other things on the concept of an Indo-Aryan linguistic family, the Aryan Race and the Golden Age of Hinduism presumably terminated by the Muslim invasions, contributed to the 'racialization' . . . of communal identity . . . through the construction and deployment of an identifiable discourse of quasi-biological, immutable differences." This portrayal of Europeans and Hindus as racial kin, and of Muslims as disparaged racial others, reflects the flexibility of constructions of race in colonial India. Baber explains that this particular configuration of race served the British well: "from the British administrators' point of view, such a discourse of a once mighty Hindu nation and race in decline provided ample ideological justification for colonialism as the indispensable agency for its eventual regeneration."[11]

In addition to classifying Hindus and Muslims, Orientalists made linguistically based racial distinctions within the Hindu population, demarcating the Aryans of the north, who spoke languages derived from Sanskrit, from the "Dravidians" of the south, who spoke non-Sanskrit-based languages such as Tamil and Telagu, as well as from the tribal peoples, who spoke what the Orientalists dubbed "Turanian" languages. Tony Ballantyne explains that this distinction created "a linguistic geography that marked off south and central India from the north. . . . Taken together, the Turanian and Dravidian peoples were a perfect foil for the definition of the characteristics of Indian Aryans." He explains that the Orientalists celebrated the Aryans as "tall, light complexioned, meat-eating monotheists" and disparaged the Turanians and Dravidians as "short, dark, vegetarian polytheists prone to idolatry and indolence."[12] Orientalists attributed the so-called decline of Hindu Aryan civilization not only to Muslim rule but also to Aryan intermarriage and intermingling with these other linguistic groups. This distinction was inflected by caste as well as by language and region. Bharat Patankar and Gail Omvedt explain that "in the 'Aryan theory of race,' the upper castes (Brahmins, Ksatriyas and Vaishyas) were thought to be descendants of early Aryan invaders while Dalits and Adivasis were described as descendants of conquered non-Aryan peoples. . . . With this went the idea of the cultural superiority of the Aryans and their dominant, if not exclusive, role in defining 'Indian' culture."[13]

As circumscribed as the brotherhood might have been, the language of fraternity and civilizational kinship permeated early colonialist accounts of British-Hindu relations. Given that the discourse of fraternity and equality are so linked, how did the Orientalists justify the political subordination of their Aryan brethren? In the Orientalist framework, the degeneration of Indian Aryan civilization made Hindus not only unfit for self-rule but also indifferent to it. The Orientalists could thus imagine that they had the tacit consent of Hindus for colonial rule. William Jones, for example, wrote to a colleague that although he might wish for "universal liberty," Hindus themselves preferred British rule to self-rule. They "are incapable of civil liberty," he wrote; "few of them have an idea of it; and those, who have, do not wish it. They must (I deplore the evil, but know the necessity of it) be ruled by an absolute power; and I feel my pain much alleviated by knowing the natives themselves as well as from observation, that they are happier under us than they were or could have been under the Sultans of Delhi or petty Rajas."[14] Jones's role in India—and, by analogy, Britain's—was to give Indians back "their" law by codifying it. Jones argued that "the natives are charmed with the work, and the idea of making their slavery lighter, by giving them their own laws, is more flattering to me than the thanks of the company and the approbation of the King which have been transmitted to me."[15] The recovery of this tradition would ensure the allegiance, in Jones's words, of the "many millions of Hindu subjects whose well directed industry would add largely to the wealth of Britain and who ask no more in return than protection for their persons and places of abode, justice in their temporal concerns, indulgence to the prejudice of their own religion, and the benefit of those laws which they have been taught to believe sacred, and which alone they can possibly comprehend."[16] According to Jones, the relationship between the colonizer and the colonized was mutually beneficial, and the consent of the colonized could be ensured if the British governed according to indigenous frameworks of law and did not interfere in religious matters.

Animated by a notion of brotherhood, then, the legitimacy of British colonial rule, according to Orientalists, rested in part on the notion that the British could rule in accordance with Indian political traditions. Producing knowledge about these traditions was thus critically important to the colonial endeavor. Warren Hastings, in his introduction to the first English translation of the *Bhagavad Gita,* wrote that "every accumulation of knowledge, and especially such as is obtained by social communication with people over whom we exercise a dominion founded on the right of conquest, is useful to the state. . . . It attracts and conciliates distant affections; it lessens the weight of the chain by which the natives are held in subjection."[17] Hastings acknowledges the role of force and conquest in the relationship between the colonizer and the colonized, but in his view the possibility of learning about and applying indigenous tradition could engender consent to British rule.

As Britain's first governor-general of India, Hastings developed a legal framework as part of the task of consolidating the East India Company's holdings in India. As part of this framework, Hastings issued a decree in 1772 that distinguished between a system of criminal law and a system of "personal law" regarding family, caste, and religious matters. By declaring the *shastras* the basis of Hindu personal law and the Koran the law applicable to Muslims, Hastings oversaw the creation of a legal system that elevated textual law over customary law, whereas custom had traditionally overridden written law.[18] In defense of his legal framework, Hastings argued that distinguishing personal from civil and criminal law constituted a policy of noninterference and would shield the British from accusations of tyrannical rule.[19] Far from noninterference, however, the legal framework developed under the Orientalists significantly bolstered the intertwined hierarchies of caste and gender.

The Orientalists' legal framework had a very significant impact on caste and gender relations. According to Thomas Trautmann, the Orientalists were a small group of British male scholars who studied "the learning of male Brahmins in Sanskrit . . . not the culture of Indians generally."[20] One of the most influential texts for the early colonial administrators was William Jones's 1794 translation from the Sanskrit of the ancient text the *Manusmirti*, or *The Laws of Manu*. The *Manusmirti* contains, among other things, commentary on the origins of the caste system and extremely conservative prescriptions for caste and gender relations. Madhu Kishwar writes that the text "influenced orientalist studies in the west far more than it had ever influenced the administration of law in pre-British India."[21] Indeed, Nicholas Dirks, in *Castes of Mind,* explains that the *Manusmirti* achieved the status of an "'applied' legal document only under early British rule." The importance that the British gave to this text, Dirks notes, "encapsulated British attempts to codify not just law but also social relations in a single, orthodox 'Hindu'—and therefore necessarily 'Brahmanic'—register."[22] Flavia Agnes notes that for more than two thousand years the trend in India and elsewhere in the region had been to "gravitate away from the structure of Brahminical superiority and Sanskrit orthodoxy," but British policy reversed that trend.[23]

In addition to consolidating hierarchical caste relations, British legal policy had a devastating impact on women's legal position in India. By designating matters of marriage, divorce, and inheritance as religious matters outside the scope of political authority, for example, Hastings's decree linked masculinist power with religious autonomy. J. Duncan Derrett examines the masculinist alignment of British and Indian legal assumptions and interests in the designation of these matters as subject to personal law, arguing that the policy reflects both the "influence of the local jurists on the representatives" and the predisposition of Hastings and his colleagues to see such matters in terms of the contemporary English division of law, in which "marriage, divorce, and inheritance questions as well as questions of religious worship were decided by ecclesiastical courts."[24] Orientalists thus ignored, or vilified as "backward," the many political and legal traditions and customs of reformist sects, lower castes, and tribal peoples.[25] Indeed, Hastings's decree set in motion what Flavia Agnes calls "the process of Brahminization and Islamization of laws" in which local practices and customs—many of them more favorable to women than the textual laws endorsed by the British, especially in the area of property relations—were displaced.[26] The British also introduced their own masculinist biases in their translations and interpretations of the ancient legal texts on which they based the legal system. Uma Chakravarti calls this interaction a "patriarchal circuit" in which the Orientalists' own masculinist beliefs were reinforced by those of the male Brahmin pundits (religious scholars) whom the British employed for guidance in interpreting the ancient texts of India, which themselves contained patriarchal assumptions.[27] This was especially damaging to women's relatively liberal rights to property ownership in Bengal, which were significantly curtailed by the British. Finally, the policy fixed a legal tradition that had been fluid and shifting. The codification of Hindu and Muslim law in accordance with ancient texts meant that the evolution of law stagnated because there was no mechanism by which it could be adapted to new circumstances. This led, in pre-independence India, to "a legal system that grew increasingly conservative and incapable of responding to social change," as Leslie Calman explains; "for women, the result was the promotion of a rigid, outmoded religious orthodoxy."[28]

The extent to which Orientalist legal policy, though cast as noninterventionist, bolstered masculinist domination can be seen in the formulation of early British decisions regarding *sati*, the practice in which a widowed woman would immolate herself on the funeral pyre of her deceased husband. In *Contentious Traditions*, Lata Mani explicates the dynamic of knowledge production regarding this practice. She explains that the information-gathering process was initiated by colonial administrators who asked pundits in residence at the provincial court whether the Hindu scriptures permitted the practice. In response to the administrators' request, the pundits highlighted passages in the scriptures that celebrated the rewards of *sati* to widows and their husbands but noted that the texts did not prescribe such a practice, only permitted it. Through this process, the court concluded that "the practice, generally speaking, being thus recognized and encouraged by the doctrines of the Hindoo religion, it appears evident that the course which the British government should follow, according to the principles of religious tolerance . . . is to allow the practice in those cases in which it is countenanced by their religion; and to prevent it in others in which it is by the same authority prohibited." This exchange resulted in an 1813 circular allowing voluntary *sati* that became the basis for colonial policy on *sati* until the practice was banned in 1829. Mani directs her readers to two crucial discursive moves in this process. First, the status of scripture in Hinduism was misperceived as "prescriptive and normative" and was elevated above custom, and second, "permission by inference [was] transformed into scriptural recognition and encouragement of sati." Acknowledging that the scriptural text was not definitive and that the pundits' analysis of the text was only an interpretation, according to Mani, would have been "incompatible with the project of the colonial state which sought to develop an exact science of ruling, which was in turn dependent on precise knowledges." Mani argues that, far from elucidating the true meaning and place of *sati* in Hinduism, official discourse *produced* a "specifically colonial" concept of sati.[29]

There is also evidence that the increase in the practice of *sati* over the course of the nineteenth century was in part a product of the colonial relationship itself. Radha Kumar finds evidence of this connection in the fact that "the only example we have of a widespread incidence of sati is in the early decades of the nineteenth century in Bengal, where there seemed to have been more than one incidence of sati a day," and she notes that the practice was most prevalent among the urban Brahmins who were in closest contact with the British colonialists.[30] Even at the time, many observers attributed the increase in the practice of *sati* to the influence of the 1813 circular, which authorized and publicized the practice on the basis of scripture.[31] Ashis Nandy characterizes this "epidemic" of *sati* as "an anxiety response to colonial rule by the colonized" and attributes it to three factors: the breakdown of traditional measures of virtue as a result of the colonial encounter, the relatively liberal Bengali inheritance laws of the time, which gave women, as wives and mothers, a right to property that upper-caste Hindu men might try to avoid, and the "social non-interventionism during the first phase of the Raj [that] seemed to many a direct endorsement of the practice." Nandy attributes the noninterventionist policy of the British with respect to the practice of *sati* in the early part of their rule to a colonial "lack of self-confidence."[32]

Far from marking a lack, however, British legal policy with respect to *sati* was congruent with imperialist ends in several ways. First, the process of knowledge production and policy formulation about *sati* solidified the close link between colonial administrator and pundit. Second, it advanced the notion of an authentic Hindu tradition that could be located in ancient scripture. To the extent to which the British followed the dictates of this tradition, they could claim that they were legitimately administering people's own laws (while bypassing the need to consult the people themselves). Finally, the policy secured masculinist power in the sense that the practice of *sati* involved questions of gendered property relations as well as issues of marriage and widowhood: Women who committed *sati* could neither make claims on the property of their deceased husbands nor remarry.

Feminist scholars have noted the role of colonialism in degrading or exacerbating hierarchical gender relations in many contexts. In some instances the colonizing state introduced a notion of gender as a binary, biologically based category in places where such differentials had not existed before.[33] In others, the colonial state actively dismantled egalitarian gender relations.[34] In India, the British consolidated both gender and caste hierarchies by choosing and imposing as law particularly inegalitarian practices and traditions over egalitarian ones. Taken together, these three processes of colonial gender transformation—introducing notions of biologically based gender where there were none, dismantling egalitarian gender relations, and choosing inegalitarian practices over egalitarian ones—can be understood as strategies by which the colonial state in general works to introduce or enhance masculinist power among the colonized. For the colonizers, this strategy has the benefit of giving colonized men themselves a stake in colonial rule, compensating them for their loss of political power with increased control within the family. Attention to fraternalism as an approach to colonial rule underscores that this mode of dominance is not "natural" or "traditional" but rather is strategically imposed.

Policies aimed at increasing masculinist power not only encouraged acquiescence in colonial rule but also contained gender dissent in the West. One of the potential effects of the colonial encounter more generally was to expose people to new modes of social organization and relations, an exposure that threatened to denaturalize the gender hierarchy in general and thus call into question gender relations within the metropole. Eradicating, disparaging, or covering up non-gender-based or more egalitarian modes of social organization neutralized this possibility by stifling potential points of contrast and contradiction. Flavia Agnes, for example, links the increase in legal constraints on women's property under the British in India to the subordinate status of women in England, where women obtained the right to own property only in 1882, and where married women had restricted transactional power over property until the twentieth century.[35] To the extent that it obscured alternatives that were neutral or egalitarian in terms of gender, fraternalist legal policy thus bolstered masculinist authority in the colony and helped to secure such authority at home.

In her study of the Orientalists in India, Jenny Sharpe notes that although attention is often focused on colonial rhetoric that disparages indigenous civilizations, discourses of "sympathy and identity" can be equally constitutive of colonialist discourse.[36] Undergirded by force and animated by an ideological rhetoric of kinship and tacit consent, the Orientalists also drew upon a politics of compensatory domination to build support for colonial rule by consolidating caste, class, religious, and gender hierarchies. This approach, one that obscured more egalitarian social relations and practices within and between communities in India, was particularly seductive in that it combined the rhetoric of validation and identification with policies that augmented caste, religious, class, and gender power. The "tradition" that the Orientalists advanced, however, was distorted and deeply shaped by colonial intervention and the alliances that the Orientalists built—and solidified caste hierarchies, exacerbated communal cleavages, increased the economic holdings of the elite, and increased masculinist control over women—and it came at the cost of submission to colonial rule itself. Ironically, it was this fictive tradition and these costly collaborations that would become the object of paternalist ire.

"NOW THAT WE ARE SUPREME": ANGLICISTS AND THE POLITICS OF COLONIAL PATERNALISM

By the 1820s, the Orientalist approach to colonial rule had been overshadowed by the growing influence of colonial scholar-administrators who would come to be known as Anglicists, so called for their assertion of the supremacy of English civilization. Prominent among these scholar-administrators were Charles Grant (1746–1823), who served as chairman of the British East India Company, James Mill (1773–1836), who wrote the extremely influential *History of British India* and served as a colonial administrator in the London office of the East India Company, and William Bentinck (1774–1839), the governor-general of India from 1828 to 1835. In contrast to Orientalist celebrations of Hindu thought and history, Anglicists characterized ancient Indian civilization as despotic and morally depraved. Accusing Orientalists of a myopic focus on ancient texts and a compromising reliance on Brahmin pundits, Anglicist scholars proposed a new colonial framework in which British administrators understood their role to be that of civilizational tutors or guides.[37] In his "Observations on the State of Society Among the Asiatic Subjects of Great Britain," Anglicist Charles Grant wrote that "the communication of our light and knowledge to them would prove the best remedy for their disorders; if this remedy is judiciously and patiently applied it would have great and happy effects upon them, effects honourable and advantageous for us."[38]

While the Orientalists emphasized the civilizational or racial links between upper-caste Hindus and the British, Anglicists denied that the linguistic kinship between European languages and Sanskrit implied a shared racial kinship. Instead, they elaborated a racial hierarchy in which skin color was linked to morality and civilization. According to Grant, for example, there was between Hindu and European morality "a difference analogous to the difference of the natural color of the two races." Grant also rejected the notion that an Aryan golden age had been disrupted by Muslim rule, instead asserting that Hindus "have had among themselves a complete despotism from the remotest antiquity" and were not degraded by Muslim rule.[39] Instead of glorifying Hindu culture and vilifying Islamic culture in India, the Anglicists disparaged both.

Although they rejected the Orientalist notion of Aryan brotherhood, the Anglicists shared with Orientalists a sense that colonial relations of rule had to be grounded in more than force if they were to be viable. Grant, for example, argued that "without a uniting principle, a conjoining tie . . . we can suppose the country to be, in fact, retained only by mere power." Given that, "at present, we are in every way different from the people whom we hold in subjection," he advocated "a principle of assimilation, a common-bond, which shall give to both parties the reality and the conviction of mutual connection." He explained that such a process of assimilation could be "healing" and would work to establish "an identity of sentiments and principles" that would enhance the government's strength by producing "a sight new in the region of Hindustan, a people actively attached" to their government.[40] Whereas the Orientalists sought to legitimate the colonial regime by an appeal to racialized fraternal solidarity, the Anglicists sought to gain support through the process of assimilating Indians to British norms and values.

In addition to discrediting the notion of a linguistically based racial fraternity between Aryan Indians and Europeans, Anglicists decried the role of the British East India Company in preserving indigenous antagonisms and hierarchies rather than challenging them. In contrast to the accommodationist approach of the Orientalists, Anglicist colonial administrators sought, according to Gyanendra Pandey, "to promote a picture of the colonial state as a wise and neutral power, ruling . . . by the sheer force of its moral authority."[41] Anglicist scholarship portrayed the relationship between Hindu and Muslim communities as marked by enduring tension, conflict, and antagonism, which required that the colonial government play the role of neutral arbiter between them. Further, Anglicists critiqued the caste bias of Orientalist writings, accusing Orientalist scholars of a damning dependence on self-serving Brahmins. Charles Grant, for example, asked, "Are we bound for ever to preserve all the enormities in the Hindoo system? Have we become the guardians of every monstrous principle and practice which it contains?"[42] Similarly, James Mill argued that the caste system was a particularly odious feature of Hindu life, asserting that with "the division of the people into castes, and the prejudices which the detestable views of the Brahmans raised to separate them, a degrading and pernicious system of subordination was established among the Hindus, and the vices of such a system were there carried to a more destructive height than among any other people."[43] Ironically, Mill's critique of caste and gender relations was based heavily on a reading of William Jones's translation of the *Manusmirti.* Nicholas Dirks explains that Mill "merely rehearsed his view of the rudeness of Hindu society and polity rather than the limits of the textual version of the position of Brahmans in society."[44]

For the Anglicists, the Indian treatment of women was another crucial marker of difference between colonizer and colonized, and the relations between the sexes an area in which the colony was most in need of paternal guidance. One of the primary goals of James Mill's *History of British India* was to "ascertain the true state of the Hindus in the scale of civilization," and he saw the status of women as the primary marker of civilizational progress. According to Mill, India fared quite badly on this score, for "nothing can exceed the habitual contempt which the Hindus entertain for their women"; "a state of dependence more strict and humiliating than that which is ordained for the weaker sex among the Hindus cannot easily be conceived."[45] Here, Mill used the allegedly tyrannical exercise of male power as justification for colonial intervention.

The publication, in 1817, of Mill's *History of British India* had important ramifications for subsequent colonial policy in India. According to Javed Majeed, Mill's text "shaped a theoretical basis for the liberal programme to emancipate India from its own culture."[46] Burton Stein writes that under the Anglicists, the British colonial policy of cultural "non-interference" shifted toward policies of "reform" and "improvement."[47] Among the most pressing policy goals of the Anglicists was the abolition of *sati.*[48] Radha Kumar explains that the British during this period considered *sati* an "odious practice," a central sign of Hindu moral depravity.[49] Just as the 1813

circular permitting *sati* illuminated aspects of the Orientalists' colonial fraternalist approach, the abolition of *sati* in the late 1820s brings into focus
crucial features of the Anglicist rhetoric of colonial paternalism.

In his official "Minute on Sati," Governor-General William Bentinck
wrote, "now that we are supreme, my opinion is decidedly in favor of an
open, avowed, and general prohibition, resting altogether upon the moral
goodness of the act and our power to enforce it."[50] Bentinck's declaration of
supremacy is symptomatic of the East India Company's officers' growing
sense that they need not rely on the kinds of enabling solidarities central
to colonial fraternalism. Burton Stein explains that "by the late 1820s, the
Company's army had succeeded in establishing a seemingly unassailable
dominance over the Indian polity that altered the nature of [their] collabora-
tive relationships with the Indian elites."[51] Although Indian reformers like
Ram Mohan Roy advocated the abolition of *sati*, others threatened that its
prohibition would lead to a withdrawal of Hindu support. In a petition sent
to the Court of Last Appeal in London, for example, the pro-*sati* lobby wrote:

> The Hindoo population of British India has always been the most
> attached . . . of Your Majesty's native subjects . . . conciliated by the tol-
> eration and protection hitherto strictly observed and exercised towards
> their religion, caste, and habits, and not, like another class of their
> native fellow-subjects [i.e., Muslims], regretting a lost domination.
> On Hindoo allegiance and fidelity the local Government [the Bengal
> presidency] have ever reposed with the most implicit and deserved
> confidence. Their solidarity composes by far the largest portion of a
> numerous and gallant army. . . . The Hindoos compose nine-tenths of
> the population of British India, and of this Presidency by far the larg-
> est proportion of men of wealth, of intelligence, of enterprise, and of
> knowledge . . . who with one voice implore the abrogation of the first
> law which has given them serious reasons to dread that their own faith
> and their own laws will no longer be preserved to them inviolable.[52]

The pro-*sati* petition was denied and the practice was outlawed in 1829;
many see its abolition as decisive evidence of a shift from Orientalist to
Anglicist predominance in the colonial administration. No longer "compromised" by dependence on what the Anglicists now saw as the disabling
solidarities of the Orientalist administrators, British rule could be legitimated on the merit of their own, to quote Bentinck, "moral goodness."[53]

Even while disparaging the communal, caste, and gender alliances of
the Orientalists, the Anglicists followed the Orientalists' lead in basing

their arguments against *sati* on appeals to scriptural sources. According to Lata Mani, for example, whereas the Orientalists saw *sati* as a practice sanctioned by religious scripture, Anglicists tended to argue that "prohibition of widow immolation was consonant with enforcing the truest principles of 'Hindu' religion."[54] James Mill attributed this disparity in readings of Hindu scripture to the compromising proximity of the Orientalists to their subject matter and their long stay in India, whereas, he wrote, "one gets from the distance and great height of Britain a superior sight of India, more complete and balanced than one gets in India itself." In his view, what was important in the discernment of Indian history and philosophy was not interaction with Indian people or knowledge of Indian languages but rather the exercise of "the powers of combination, discrimination, classification, judgment, comparison, weighing, inferring, inducting [and] philosophizing," which "are the powers of most importance for extracting the precious ore from a great mine of rude historical materials."[55]

In her celebrated essay "Can the Subaltern Speak?" Gayatri Spivak notes that the campaign against *sati* was rhetorically cast as "white men saving brown women from brown men."[56] For the Anglicists, protecting women justified incursions into realms deemed under the sphere of religious authority. The decree abolishing *sati* affirmed, for example, "one of the first and most important principles of the system of British government in India, that all classes of people be secure in the observance of their religious usages"—but only "so long as that system can be adhered to without violation of the paramount dictates of justice and humanity."[57] Uma Chakravarti explains that, for the imperialists, the degeneration of Hindu civilization and the abject position of Hindu women required "the 'protection' and 'intervention' of the colonial state."[58] If control over women served as compensation for colonial domination under the Orientalists, the Anglicists used such control as justification for colonial intervention. Colonial administrators understood the framework of colonial paternalism to be to the supposed moral benefit of the Indians, in line with the "truest" principles of religious ethics, again with women as a central term of political exchange.

Although seemingly opposed, the logic of fraternalist and paternalist approaches to colonial rule worked together to enable colonial rule in interlocking ways. First, the fraternalism of Orientalist scholarship and policy helped shape the "traditional" practices and hierarchies that were the object of paternalist outrage. Second, although one approach or the other might have been rhetorically dominant, both approaches were often concurrently pursued. As Lata Mani points out, although James Mill regarded the implementation of indigenous law as "an aspect of the mercantilist and extractive character of the East India Company and its monopoly privileges," when it came to the law, he simply "reiterated the position the East India company had pursued since 1792 'with such modifications as not to shock the prejudices and manners of the people, and with all the authority which the brahmanical character and the most sacred names could attach to it.'"[59] Further, despite their rhetoric about protecting widows in the campaign against *sati*, the judicial decisions made during the period when Anglicists were ascendant continued to erode women's transactional power over their property. Agnes explains that "while it was relatively easy to pose as 'rescuers' of Indian women from the clutches of 'barbaric' customs like sati and infant marriages, it was indeed not easy to conciliate with the notions of civil right of property ownership which was a contentious issue in Britain at the time. These notions were adopted into the Indian system, even while posturing to liberate women from the 'barbaric' customs through legislative reforms."[60]

Fraternalist and paternalist approaches could also be alternated to contain dissent, depending on the specific context. After the mutiny of 1857, for example, colonial administrators tried to reinstate the earlier terms of the fraternalist colonial rule. Mrinalini Sinha explains that the mutiny

> eroded much of the early nineteenth-century confidence in the Anglicist programme. The expression of Indian discontent in 1857 was seen as a warning against the radical restructuring of "traditional" Indian society. The suppression of the rebellion and the transfer of India from the East India Company to the British Crown in 1858 ushered in a new era of caution: the colonial administrators henceforth sought allies in the traditional landholding classes and orthodox religious leaders who were seen as the main forces behind the rebellion of 1857. . . . The mid-century Anglicist perspective began to be tempered by a revival of the Orientalist perspective.[61]

This policy was reflected in legislative quiescence on matters relating to the "woman question" and in the reinstatement of legally permissible "voluntary" *sati* in the Indian Penal Code of 1860.[62]

Finally, both approaches generated alliances that helped to foster British rule. While the fraternalist approach depended on the collaboration of elite groups, colonial paternalism depended on the support of those both within and outside of India who hoped to put the colonial state in the service of reform. Included in the latter category were "imperialist feminists" such as the American Katherine Mayo, the author of the infamous *Mother India*, who argued that colonial rule was necessary for the protection of Indian women. The irony, of course, is that these reformers turned to the state that helped to generate these hierarchies and that had its own stake (sometimes submerged) in their continuation.

In *The Racial Contract*, Charles Mills writes that the colonial contract is an important subcontract of the racial contract. It is the colonial contract, he explains, that helped legitimate the modern world as a "racial polity, globally dominated by the Europeans."[63] Although Mills refers to the colonial contract in the singular, in this chapter I have argued that that there were two distinct articulations of the colonial contract in India and that the lenses of fraternalism and paternalism reveal the shifting justificatory logic and enabling collaborations on which colonial projections of "consent" depended.

Given that both Orientalist and Anglicist policies served the ends of imperial rule, Mani concludes that it is important not to overdraw the differences between the two approaches: "Even the most vigorous reformers in Britain opted for caution, if not reluctance, when it came to the colonies," she writes. "The colonial state was fundamentally defined by its appropriative relationship to indigenous society, and only those reforms were contemplated that in no way interrupted the logic of accumulation. . . . The shift from Orientalist praise to Anglicist condemnation was thus primarily a transformation in attitude."[64] While Orientalist and Anglicist policies did serve similar ends, their distinct logics, policies, and rhetoric, as I show in the following chapter, meant that freedom fighters in India had to adopt differing strategies in order to contest British imperial rule successfully.

COLONIAL SCHOLARSHIP AND COMPARATIVE POLITICAL THEORY

Before turning to another chapter in Indian history, however, I want to conclude with a few thoughts on the implications of the interplay between fraternalism and paternalism in colonial rule for political theorizing more generally. As we work toward an anticolonialist political theory, what lessons can be gleaned from the role that British knowledge production in India played in colonial rule?

In *Unthinking Eurocentrism*, Ella Shohat and Robert Stam write that "Eurocentrism is the discursive residue or precipitate of colonialism, the process by which the European powers reached positions of economic, military, political and cultural hegemony in much of Asia, Africa, and the

Americas."[65] Although the field of political theory in the West has been long marked by Eurocentrism, a promising contemporary development is the emergence of the subfield of comparative political theory. One of the strengths of this subfield is its explicit rejection of the politics of paternalist Eurocentrism. From Anthony Parel's comparison of the baleful effects of Eurocentric political theory to a poisonous Upas tree, to Uday Singh Mehta's call for "conversations across boundaries of strangeness" that are animated with "imaginative humility," scholars of comparative political theory have been consistently critical of the power relations enabled by Eurocentrism.[66] If colonialism, as Shohat and Stam assert, "is ethnocentrism armed, institutionalized and gone global," such shifts in epistemological orientation and animation are crucial to building anti-Eurocentric political theories that can contribute to an anti-imperial politics.[67] Indeed, Fred Dallmayr asserts that the goal of comparative political theory is "to replace or supplement the rehearsal of routinized canons with a turn to global, cross-cultural or comparative political theorizing [in which] in contrast to hegemonic and imperialist modes of theorizing, one segment of the world's population [would not] monopolize the language or idiom of the emerging global civil society."[68]

Attention to India's colonial history reveals, however, that paternalism is not the only epistemological trap to avoid in building an anticolonialist political theory. Indeed, in contrast to paternalism's Eurocentrism, fraternalism is polycentric in its cross-cultural engagement and is often celebratory of other philosophies and cultures.[69] As such, it can seem an enticing alternative to Eurocentrism. But fraternalism is no less implicated in the destruction and degradation of other knowledges and ways of being than paternalism, only differently so. While paternalist Eurocentrism ignores or disparages non-Western knowledge *in general,* fraternalist polycentrism embraces *some* indigenous knowledge and practices over others, in particular those that embrace power and hierarchy over those that are grounded in more egalitarian assumptions or practices. An antifraternalist approach to comparative political theory would investigate the ways in which particular modes of cross-cultural knowledge production have been used to consolidate gender, racial, caste, class, and ethnic privilege. It would also involve the task of recovering those theories and practices that have been systematically downplayed or discarded.

The importance of an antifraternalist comparative political theory lies not only in challenging the marginalization and subordination of women and other nondominant groups within given societies, but also in its potential to work against cross-cultural domination. In contemporary politics, attention to the class, racial, and gender solidarities that enable the inequitable distribution of global power and resources is particularly important given that the "linchpin of neo-colonialism" in Shohat and Stam's words, "is a close alliance between foreign capital and the indigenous elite."[70] Indeed, one can find ample evidence in contemporary politics of fraternalism and paternalism as interchanging rhetorics of rule; in U.S. foreign policy, for example, witness the ways that the Bush administration emphasized the need to rescue Afghani women as a justification for military intervention in Afghanistan and then, when faced with reports that Afghani women were being prohibited from protesting, called the issue a matter of people's "own cultures and histories."[71]

Comparative political theory has the potential to make important contributions to an anticolonialist politics, particularly in this era when neocolonial interventions are done in the name and over the terms and conditions of democracy. Given these opportunities for intervention, it is important to be vigilant against the legacy and practice of fraternalism as a means by which polycentric modes of inquiry are aligned with colonialist or neocolonialist ends. In doing so, we can avoid the pitfall of replacing the Eurocentric canon with new polycentric canon that is, to echo Lata Mani, "different in attitude" yet nonetheless sustains inequitable relations of rule both within societies and between them.

Resistant Convergences: Anticolonial Feminist Nationalism

With the emergence of the struggle for Indian independance, various coalitions challenged the logic of both paternalist and fraternalist approaches to Britain's rule in India. While the previous chapter explored several of the alliances that were crucial to the generation and maintenance of colonial rule, this chapter investigates some of the coalitions that contributed to its displacement. Key among these were nationalist and feminist groups that worked together to address questions of women's legal and political subordination in a manner that both exposed the hollowness of British paternalist claims to "protect" Indian women, minority groups, and lower castes and rejected the compensatory rewards of fraternalist control over those groups.

If the politics of compensatory domination consolidates power within and between groups in patterned ways, a key aspect of the fight against subordination of the whole group is a struggle to reject the ways that the most powerful members of the group are enticed from above to dominate others within the group. Indeed, an important corollary to the work of identifying and analyzing intragroup hierarchies is highlighting points at which different struggles come together to challenge such lines of power. I call a point at which movements link to contest inequitable power relations within a subordinated group a "resistant convergence" of struggles. There were a number of moments of resistant convergence in the struggle for Indian independence—moments, for example, when men joined with women to resist gender domination, when upper-caste Hindus joined with lower-caste Hindus and members of minority religious groups to resist caste and communal domination, and when Britons and other Westerners joined with Indians to resist colonial domination.[1]

Although many stories of resistant convergence could be told, this chapter focuses primarily on the relationship between the nationalist and women's movements in their concerted efforts to enfranchise women and to enact legal reform. I argue that because colonial authorities contained dissent in part by pursuing policies and generating rhetoric that enhanced upper-caste Hindu men's gender, communal, and caste dominance, both movements' opposition to such inter- and intragroup dominance deeply undercut the legitimacy of the colonial state and destabilized conservative alliances crucial to British rule. I also look at points in the struggle for women's legal and political emancipation where efforts to resist the consolidation of intragroup hierarchies faltered—for example, in efforts to reform Hindu personal law and to increase women's voting rights and parliamentary representation. I suggest that this wavering had to do both with the Indian National Congress's efforts to "become the state, even as it was contesting the state,"[2] and with the gender, caste, and communal investments of dominant groups in the nationalist and feminist movements.

While there were certainly limits to the alliance between nationalists and feminists in the struggle for Indian independence, these groups were also able to coalesce in significant ways to challenge the consolidation of dominance and privilege. This alliance not only was significant and efficacious at the time but suggests possibilities for coalitional democratic solidarity in our own era. As partial, thwarted, and fleeting as these moments of resistant convergence sometimes were, their legacy points to the possibility and efficacy of struggles that widen and deepen a democratic transformation of relations within and between groups.

RESISTANT CONVERGENCE

Early cultural nationalists in India firmly rejected the politics of colonial paternalism, in particular its disparagement of indigenous civilization and culture, its emphasis on civilizational tutelage and assimilation, and its critique of indigenous masculinist authority. Indeed, in *The Nation and Its Fragments*, Partha Chatterjee suggests that a key moment in the struggle against British rule in India occurred in the late nineteenth century, when early nationalists silenced debate on "the woman question." Chatterjee argues that the nationalist silence on the woman question is deceptive: It did not mean that the colonizers and the colonized had reached agreement on the "woman question" but reflected the nationalists' refusal to make that issue a subject of debate with the British. Chatterjee suggests that by shutting down debate over the position of Indian women, nationalists mounted an important challenge to imperial authority: Faced with domination in the material "outer" realm (comprising such worldly matters as statecraft and economic planning), nationalists asserted their superiority in the spiritual or "inner" realm. Chatterjee explains women's symbolic association with this inner sphere: "Applying the inner/outer distinction to the matter of concrete day-to-day living separates the social space into *ghar* and *bahir,* the home and the world. . . . The home in its essence must remain unaffected by the profane activities of the material world—and woman is its representation. And so one gets an identification of social roles by gender to correspond with the separation of the social space into *ghar* and *bahir.*"[3]

Although Chatterjee focuses on the analogy between women and the home in the nationalist imaginary, feminist historians highlight the power relations that this move both reflected and produced. Kumkum Sangari and Sudesh Vaid write that by distinguishing between the home and the world, nationalists asserted a "new formation of the home as the insulated private sphere" in which masculinist control over women was consolidated.[4] Kumari Jayawardena expands on Chatterjee's argument, adding that "the home (and women) were not merely a representation of the spiritual . . . but also an area of material interest to males in terms of unpaid labor and services."[5] In refusing to debate the "woman question" with the British, Indian nationalists claimed control over women for themselves.

While the masculinist reassertion of sovereignty over the home represented a challenge to the British paternalist approach to colonial rule, it could be accommodated all too easily within a fraternalist approach to rule that strengthened and solidified masculinist control over women in exchange for their support of (or at least acquiescence in) colonial rule. As discussed in the previous chapter, the British sought to secure this acquiescence by pursuing a fraternalist hands-off policy in matters of religion and women, a move they accomplished by downplaying matters relating to the "woman question" and reinstating legally permissible "voluntary" *sati.*[6]

The story of cultural nationalist engagement in the "woman question" did not end with such a reaffirmation of colonial fraternalist policy, however. While some nationalists asserted the importance of masculinist control over women in the home as crucial to cultural autonomy, others opposed it strenuously. Indeed, Tanika Sarkar argues that there were two cultural nationalist approaches to Hindu domestic practices and custom in the late nineteenth century: the approach discussed above, which held that household relations were an "excess reserved over and above colonization,

any change in which would signify the surrender of the last bastion of freedom," and the approach that held that household relations were deeply
distorted by colonial rule.[7] Proponents of the second view challenged the
notion of control over women as compensation for colonial subordination.
For some reformers, masculinist domination was a wholly inadequate form
of compensation for what had been lost and served only to highlight the
perversity of colonial domination. As one commentator put it, "when our
white masters kick us, we return home and soothe ourselves by kicking our
wives." Another described the subordination of women as an added cost of
colonial rule and lamented the ways in which, as he put it, "our women lost
their freedom when we lost ours."[8]

Moreover, women themselves began to question their subordination in
an organized way. Indeed, as the historian Geraldine Forbes observes, if
the "woman question" seemed to be settled at the end of the nineteenth
century, women themselves opened it at the beginning of the twentieth.
According to Forbes, women's associations with the goal of "bringing
together women to discuss women's issues . . . sprang up all over India in
the late nineteenth and early twentieth centuries" and enabled women to
"define their own interests, propose solutions, and take action." Between
1917 and 1927, three major national organizations were formed with
branches throughout India: the Women's Indian Association (WIA), the
National Council of Women in India, and the All-India Women's Conference (AIWC).[9] Together, these groups formed the national infrastructure
of the burgeoning women's movement in India and served as networks of
communication, mobilization, and protest. In addition to becoming active
members of these groups, Muslim women formed the All-India Muslim
Women's Conference in 1907, the Anjuman-e-Khwateen-Deccan in 1919,
and numerous "*purdah* clubs" where women could meet and discuss issues
of concern. These groups focused on issues such as education, *purdah*
(from the Urdu for "curtain," purdah is the practice of preventing women
from being seen by men), raising the age of marriage, and polygamy, often
arguing that the failure to implement women's Islamic rights led to practices that discriminated against women.[10]

Although most women's groups of this period initially limited their
interests to the supposedly "nonpolitical" issues of women's education and
social uplift, they soon made the connection between the anti-imperialist
struggle and women's emancipation. Nivedita Menon traces the AIWC's
analytical trajectory, writing that it "was set up to discuss the issue of female
education, but it soon found this question could not be addressed without
looking at other issues such as purdah and child-marriage. From here came

the realization that these questions could not be separated from India's political subjection. Thus, the AIWC came to a point where it stressed the political goal of national self-government to achieve women's aspirations."[11] The AIWC and the other leading women's groups linked women's emancipation to national liberation. By embracing the goal of national self-government, the women's movement thus rejected terms of colonial paternalism that held up the colonial state as the protector of women.

The early twentieth century was also marked by the growth of support for gender rights in the different strands of the Indian nationalist movement. Margaret Cousins, an Irish suffragist who worked for national independence and women's rights in India, wrote that "from the beginning [the enthusiasm for political freedom] was linked with a realization that it should be freedom for women as well as for men."[12] Gandhi himself wrote that if nationalists believed that "freedom is the birthright of every nation and individual . . . [they should] first liberate their women from the evil customs and conventions that restrict" them, adding, "to postpone social reform till after the attainment of Swaraj [i.e., home rule], is not to know the meaning of Swaraj."[13] This commitment was institutionalized in several ways. From its inception in 1885, for example, membership in the Indian National Congress (INC) was open to women. Furthermore, there was significant overlap in the leadership of the nationalist and feminist movements. In 1925, for example, Sarojini Naidu became the first Indian-born woman to serve as president of the INC; she became president of the AIWC three years later.

The early twentieth century also saw the rise of autonomous Muslim organizations in the struggle for Indian independence (although many Muslims joined the INC as well). Most prominent among these organizations was the Muslim League. Formed in 1906, the Muslim League rejected the colonial paternalist notion that British rule was necessary to mediate antagonisms between Hindus and Muslims, yet it was also wary of the possibility that a Hindu electoral majority would overwhelm the interests of a Muslim minority in an independent India. To work against that outcome, the Muslim League pursued a variety of measures that would ensure Muslim political access and representation, among them separate electorates, reserved seats, territorial grouping, and (ultimately) the partition of India and Pakistan. The Muslim League supported gender rights and established women's branches throughout the country. Muslim League leaders like Muhammad Ali Jinnah and the Nizam of Hyderbad publicly supported the stance of women's groups on *purdah* and passed resolutions in favor of women's suffrage, representation, and social equality. Seema

Kazi explains that "the recognition of the importance of women's issues by the national leadership contributed towards strengthening the women's movement as a whole."[14]

Just as many Muslims feared the prospect of Hindu domination in an independent India, many low-caste groups, called Dalits (oppressed) or untouchables, feared upper-caste domination. To many Dalits, life under British rule seemed preferable to what might become unchecked rule by the upper castes. Two of the most important sections of the anticaste movement, one led by B. R. Ambedkar and the other dubbed the "Self-Respect Movement," however, rejected the logic that the British were able protectors of Dalit rights. Ambedkar argued that despite colonial rhetoric to the contrary, "Our wrongs have remained as open sores and they have not been righted, although 150 years of British rule have rolled away. Of what good is such a government to anybody?" Instead, he suggested, only in an independent India could Dalits and low-caste groups achieve justice. In one speech to fellow Dalits he asserted that "it is only in a *swaraj* constitution that you stand any chance of getting political power . . . without which you cannot bring salvation to our people."[15]

In southern India, members of non-Brahman communities initiated the Dravidian movement by forming the Justice Party in 1916.[16] This party agitated against upper-caste domination in the nationalist movement, arguing that independence from England would only lead to further Brahman domination of the south and advocating instead for increased non-Brahman representation in a British administration. Although the Justice Party succeeded in gaining representation for non-Brahmans in the legislature, it languished in the early 1920s, as support for independence grew in southern India and the Justice Party's ties with the British government came to be seen as suspect.[17] The Justice Party was revived through the leadership of E. V. Ramasami, reverently referred to as "Periyar," who in 1925 broke with the Indian National Congress Party after a Brahman ousted him from his position as president of the Tamilnad Congress Committee.[18] Periyar reinvigorated the flagging Dravidian movement by combining opposition to both the British and Brahmans in what became known as the Self-Respect Movement. In a pamphlet explaining the goals of the movement, Periyar wrote, "those who are for freedom today are neglecting self-respect. . . . Without self-respect there will be no good of freedom. We want a *swaraj* . . . where there will be no exploitation of any kind."[19] For Periyar, non-Brahman identity was coextensive with Dravidian identity, and a reform of caste practices would lead to a rejuvenation of Dravidian culture. According to Jacob Pandian, Periyar's "main thesis was

that Brahmans had debased Dravidian culture . . . [and that] in order to sal-
vage Dravidian culture from its impure state, Brahmanical priesthood and
Sanskritic scriptural tradition must be destroyed."[20] In making this argument, Periyar turned colonial racial historiography on its head: Instead
of the Aryans being degraded by their interaction with the indigenous
peoples of India, the indigenous cultures were debased by their encounter
with hierarchical Aryan culture.

In addition to challenging colonial racial historiography, the anticaste
movement called attention to the close links between gender subordination and caste exploitation. Ambedkar, for example, argued that since caste
"purity" hinged on the practices of endogamy, gender and caste were deeply
bound up with each other. In his view, since the caste system required strict
control over women's sexuality, Brahmanism engendered practices such as
"sati, enforced widowhood and child marriage . . . in order to regulate and
control any transgression of boundaries." Given this linkage between gender rules and caste rules, he argued, "women are the gateways to the caste
system." Reflecting his commitment to destroying both caste and gender
as linked systems of domination, Ambedkar would organize a women's
conference as part of every general meeting that he called.[21] In addition to
being supported by the leadership, Dalit women began to organize independent meetings and conference in the 1930s.

Periyar and the Self-Respect Movement stressed that the disadvantaged
position of women was a result of Brahman dominance in the south. The
Self-Respect League took up questions of gender justice as central to its struggle against upper-caste Hindu domination in nationalist politics. C. S. Lakshmi writes that women were very involved in the Self-Respect League and
"gave fiery speeches against religion and men who enslave women."[22] In
addition to advocating social reforms such as the right of widows to remarry
and the abolition of child marriage, the Self-Respect League popularized a
form of egalitarian marriage that did not require Brahmans as officiators.
These "self-respect" marriages dispensed with the priest and Hindu ritual
and instead selected an officiator, without consideration of caste, from those
attending the ceremony. Both partners in the marriage pledged that "whatever rights I demand from you, I am willing to give you the same." The self-
respect marriages became symbols of an egalitarianism that had been lost
with the imposition of Brahmanic law under colonial rule.

As these examples illustrate, the relationship between the women's
movement and the different strands of the nationalist movement in India
was marked by moments of resistant convergence, moments, that is,
when the struggle for independence involved contesting the hierarchies

consolidated by the British on the basis of gender, caste, and religion. As I discuss below, this resistant convergence was especially evident in the campaign for women's suffrage, as well as in the struggle to end child marriages by raising the age of consent. In these campaigns, members of both movements backed up the other's campaigns in critical, mutually reinforcing ways and thus profoundly disrupted the logic of colonial fraternalism by calling into question the conservative alliances upon which British rule depended and upending the equation of masculinist control over women with autonomy.

The campaign for women's suffrage illustrates well the capacity of the women's and the nationalist movements to work together to challenge gendered power relations, and it demonstrates the disruptive effects of such a resistant convergence on the colonial project more broadly. Although late nineteenth-century reforms had given the franchise to propertied men in India under British rule, women (and, indeed, most men) were denied the vote. In 1917, however, the British secretary of state for India, Edwin Montagu, embarked on a mission to draw up a new Indian constitution with the intention of increasing the franchise. An all-female fourteen-member "votes for women" delegation met with Montagu and presented him with a petition that outlined their position. The petition itself illustrates three discursive moves key to the resistant convergence of the two movements. First, the delegates proclaimed their allegiance to the goals of nationalist self-determination, explaining that "the women of India understand and support the broad claims of their people for self-government within the Empire and they press for its bestowal as urgently as do their brothers."[23] This declaration of support for nationalist goals simultaneously gestured toward the alignment of the nationalist and the women's movements and asserted the women's groups' rejection of the paternalist logic that the colonial state was necessary to protect women.

The petition also presented the delegation's demand for suffrage, requesting that "when the franchise is being drawn up, women may be recognized as 'people' and that it may be worded in such terms as will not disqualify our sex, but allow our women the same opportunities of representation as our men." With this move the delegates refused to be marginalized on the basis of their gender and thus rejected the logic of colonial fraternalism on this point. Finally, the delegation asserted that nationalist men backed the struggle for women's suffrage, explaining that "the precedent for including women in modern Indian political life has been a marked feature of the Indian National Congress, in which, since its inception, women have voted and been delegates and speakers, and which this year finds its climax in the election of a woman [Besant] as its President. Thus the voice of India approves of its women being considered responsible and acknowledged citizens."[24] In this way the delegates emphasized that nationalist support of women's suffrage could be gauged by the openness of the INC to women's participation and leadership and that through their involvement in nationalist politics, women were prepared to take an active role in the political life of country.

Although the women's delegation presented him with the assurance of male support, Montagu ignored this argument and instead emphasized that Indian men opposed the extension of the vote to women. His diary entry that day offers a revealing account of the dynamics of colonial fraternal alliance building:

> We had an interesting deputation from the women, asking for education for girls, more medical colleges, etc. etc. . . . . They asked also for women's votes. . . . They assured me that the Congress would willingly pass a unanimous request for women's suffrage. Immediately [after] they had gone we interviewed the Coorg Landholder's association, who want very moderate reforms in Coorg. . . . I asked them if there were any women landholders in Coorg. They said: Yes. I asked if they were members of their association. They said: No. I asked why. They said it had never occurred to them. I argued in favour of women's suffrage, and one man blurted out fiercely: "Yes, but women are women," which seemed to him to conclude the whole subject.[25]

Montagu presents himself here as an advocate of women's suffrage bound by indigenous opposition to such reform. In order to maintain this stance he had to downplay the women's groups' assurance of indigenous male support for female suffrage. Although Montagu portrays himself as a liberal in favor of expanding the franchise, he opposed its extension to women on the grounds that it might provoke conservatives.

Montagu's meeting with the Coorg landholders and his subsequent recommendation against women's suffrage exemplify the centrality of conservative alliances to colonial decision-making processes on issues of social reform, and the extent to which, paternalist rhetoric notwithstanding, the colonial state could not be counted on to support women's struggles for political rights. Indeed, in her chronicle of the early days of the woman's movement in India, feminist and nationalist activist Kamaladevi Chattopadhyaya noted that one of the features that distinguished the women's suffrage campaign in India was the collaboration between conservative forces and the colonial state; according to Chattopadhyaya, "the fight of progress . . . is not merely against conservatism but also against the state which undoubtedly favours, in its own interest, the continuance of reactionary forces."[26]

Disheartened but not defeated by Montagu's report, women's groups moved to shore up support for women's suffrage within the nationalist movement. When the thirty-third session of the Indian National Congress met in Delhi in 1918, Saraladevi Chaudhurani presented it with a resolution supporting the vote for women, asserting that "the sphere of women" included "comradeship with men in the rough and tumble of life and to being the fellow workers of men in politics and other spheres."[27] The INC passed the resolution easily. The Muslim League passed a similar resolution the same year.[28]

The next opportunity women's groups had to present their case for women's suffrage came with the formation of the Southborough Franchise Committee, an investigative body created to make recommendations for the expansion of the franchise.[29] Representatives from women's groups throughout the country met with the committee and testified in support of extending the franchise to women. When the Southborough Committee issued its report in April 1919, however, it again recommended against extending the franchise, arguing that it would be "out of harmony with the conservative feeling of the country" and adding, "we are satisfied that the social conditions of India make it premature to extend the franchise to Indian women at this juncture, when so large a proportion of male electors require education in the use of a responsible vote. . . . Further, until the custom of seclusion of women, followed by many classes and communities, is relaxed, female suffrage would hardly be a reality."[30] Women's groups were infuriated. Muthulakshmi Reddi argued that "the British government in my opinion and in the opinion of the majority of our men and women, has not been helping our moral and social progress and has been adopting a policy of utter indifference, neutrality, and sometimes direct opposition to all our social reform measures." Margaret Cousins concurred, noting that the British were seeking at once to portray "Indian conditions [as] behind the times, Indian women [as] lagging behind all other women," while at the same time ensuring through legislation that women and India "will remain behind the times."[31] Cousins's and Reddi's analyses underscore the extent to which relations of colonial rule depended on, even while decrying, the subordination of women.

In response to the Franchise Committee's report, women's groups held large public protests, organized telegram campaigns, and sent a delegation to England to testify against the recommendation before the Joint

Parliamentary Committee, the body in charge of finalizing the reports into the government of India bill. As a result of these protests, coupled with the support of members of the major nationalist organizations (the INC, the Muslim League, and the Home Rule League) and British women's groups, the struggle achieved a partial victory. Although the government of India bill did not extend the franchise to women, it did enable provincial Indian legislatures to remove sex as a restrictive category. The enfranchisement debate was thus shifted to the provinces. In the debates over women's suffrage at that level, British representatives in these legislatures again argued against women's suffrage on the grounds that it would disrupt social conventions and customs. Cousins notes that "these debates seem to vindicate the contention of Indian social reformers and INC leaders who accused the government of systematically supporting conservatism, hardening postures on social customs, and fixing conditions in Hindu society to the detriment of social progress."[32] By highlighting the ways in which British colonial administrators sought to block progressive legislation, feminists and nationalists exposed the colonial complicity in conservative formulations of social customs themselves.

With the question of women's suffrage shifted to the provincial legislatures, local governance bodies had the opportunity to call the bluff of British colonial administrators. Muthulakshmi Reddi explains the colonial logic behind placing the decision in the hands of Indian men: "They [the British] thought they were quite safe from the possibility of political freedom for Indian women through giving power into the hands of Indians themselves to deal with the question." The British, in other words, bargained that the conservative alliances of colonial fraternalism would hold. The support of provincial legislative bodies for women's suffrage, however, proved this logic faulty. In depending on Indian men to reject the legislation, Reddi asserted, the British demonstrated "how little they knew of the spirit of educated Indians and of the veneration which is accorded to Indian women."[33] Indeed, the provincial legislatures quickly passed resolutions in favor of women's suffrage, beginning with the Madras and Bombay legislatures in 1921 and followed shortly by the other legislatures. An elated Margaret Cousins proclaimed that "the status of the Indian Nation has risen even higher than that of the British people . . . for women here are enfranchised on exactly equal terms with men, while in England only women over 30 years may vote. . . . Had the question of recognizing Indian women on terms of political equality with men rested on the decision of the British Parliament, the enfranchisement of women would have been postponed on every kind of misrepresentation and ignorance and prejudice."[34]

The provincial governments' overwhelming response in favor of the franchise for women on the same terms as men—one province even made history by voting unanimously—gave the lie to British claims of protection of Indian womanhood central to colonial paternalism and deeply undercut the conservative collaborations at the heart of colonial fraternalism.

Partha Chatterjee suggests that after independence, "the new constitution gave women the vote without any major debate on the question and without there ever having been a movement for women's suffrage at any period of nationalist politics in India." Why, in his otherwise astute reading of the "woman question" and nationalism in India, does Chatterjee miss the sustained movement for women's suffrage in India? On the one hand, his dismissal of this movement can be attributed to his much criticized inattention to the extensive documentation of the women's movement in India before independence and thus his conclusion that, except for individual struggles documented in autobiographies and journals, there was a "seeming absence of any autonomous struggle by women themselves for equality and freedom."[35] On the other hand, however, by focusing primarily on the politics of colonial paternalism and its rejection by cultural nationalists, his analysis itself precludes recognition of the important ways in which the feminist and nationalist movements converged to resist colonial fraternalism as well. Without close attention to the politics of colonial fraternalism, convergence could easily be interpreted as the submergence of one struggle in the other. If there seemed to be nationalist and feminist agreement on the women's question, it was an agreement forged in opposition to colonial rule: In order to reject colonial rule successfully, nationalists and feminists had to work together to reject masculinist rule as justification or compensation for colonial intervention.

The campaign to end child marriages by raising the age of consent is another example of resistant convergence that linked the struggle for Indian independence and the struggle for gender rights. This campaign effectively refuted the argument that women's subordination in the family necessitated British rule; in the nationalist and feminist framing of the issue, gender justice meant the overthrow of British rule in India, not its continuation. The coordination of efforts by the women's and nationalist movements was key to this rhetorical reversal. After the expansion of the franchise in 1919, for example, women's organizations, in particular the WIA, began to press the legislature to reform child marriage, with the support of both the INC and the Muslim League.

This indigenous resistance to an internal gender hierarchy put the colonial government in a difficult position. No longer could it point to an uncontested masculinism as an authentic Indian tradition that justified its presence, whether in a paternalist or a fraternalist hands-off sense. On the one hand, as the historian Mrinalini Sinha notes, if the government opposed legislation such as the measure to raise the age of consent in marriage, it risked appearing "reactionary before domestic and international public opinion." On the other hand, if the government supported such legislation, it risked "alienating support from orthodox social forces in India at a time when Indian nationalism had succeeded in considerably eroding the support base of the colonial government."[36]

In response to this dilemma, the colonial government first tried to stall the child marriage legislation. When this approach failed, it recommended voting against the measure, while cautioning its representative against "conveying to the Assembly and to the world at large that we were opposed to beneficial social legislation."[37] In the face of much international and domestic pressure, however, the colonial government finally gave the legislation its support in 1929 and raised the minimum age of marriage for a girl to fourteen. However, the colonial government rarely enforced the law, known as the Sarda Act, a signal of its lackluster support for the measure. Despite this lack of enforcement, the passage of the law illustrates the power of the resistant convergence of the feminist and nationalist movements in blocking the interplay between fraternalism and paternalism and exposing the colonial stakes in the subordination of Indian women.

Even these examples of moments of successful resistant convergence were not, of course, without struggle and tension. For example, although Gandhi urged women to join the struggle for independence, the thousands of women who did so pressed for inclusion in ways that sometimes went beyond what male nationalist leaders would abide. Gandhi and leaders of the Indian National Congress initially excluded women from the 1930 salt *satyagraha* (civil disobedience campaign), in which nationalists marched to the coast and began manufacturing salt illegally. Nationalist and feminist leaders such as Kamaladevi Chattopadhyaya were infuriated and demanded to be a part of this critical campaign. In an oral history of the salt *satyagraha* campaign, she recounted that "at first . . . Gandhiji . . . had expressed his desire not to involve women in this direct action. So, when their Bombay City Program was being prepared and seven people were selected who would symbolically break the salt law, the organizers were very averse to including any women in it. Several of us pressed very much that it would look very odd, indeed, if at the start of the movement, women were excluded."[38]

Gandhi eventually agreed, and women's participation and leadership in the salt *satyagraha* and subsequent civil disobedience campaigns became pivotal to their success. According to Jawaharlal Nehru, the future prime minister of India, "so far as the national movement is concerned, the mere fact that such large numbers of women have taken such a large part in it makes it absolutely impossible for any nationalist to conceive of keeping them down in any political or social sense."[39] Furthermore, British mistreatment of women in prisons and in marches served to underscore the hypocrisy of British claims that their goal was the protection of women.

In the Karachi meeting of the Indian National Congress in 1931, the INC officially recognized the pivotal role of women in the civil disobedience campaign and affirmed its commitment to the enfranchisement of women: "This Congress congratulates all those who underwent great suffering during the Civil Disobedience campaign. . . . The Congress more specifically congratulates the women of India who rose in the thousands and assisted the nation in its struggle for freedom and respectfully assures them that no Constitution will be acceptable to the Congress that discriminates against the sex in the matter of franchise."[40] A few days later the INC issued a statement of the fundamental rights that were to be enshrined in an independent India. This statement asserted gender equality as central to the nationalist vision of swaraj. "Any constitution which may be agreed to on its behalf should provide or enable the Swaraj Government," the statement read, "to provide equal rights and obligations of all citizens without any bar on account of sex; no disability to attach to any citizen by reason of his or her religion, caste or creed or sex in regard to public employment, office of power or honour, and in the exercise of any trade or calling."[41] In this affirmation of gender equality as a fundamental right of swaraj, the equation of cultural autonomy with control over women was turned on its head: Freedom for the nation would mean political emancipation for women.

LIMITS OF CONVERGENCE

Whereas the struggles outlined above illustrate moments of successful (albeit sometimes strained) resistant convergence between the women's and nationalist movements in India, the campaigns to further reform personal laws and expand the franchise in the 1930s and 1940s demonstrate some of the limits of this alliance. Sumit Sarkar writes that the history of anti-imperialist struggles is "profoundly ambiguous and contradictory," given that as the nationalist movement, and in particular the INC, "fought against the Raj . . . it was also progressively becoming the Raj." Sarkar argues that the INC contained the more radical possibilities of the anti-imperialist movement by simultaneously mobilizing subaltern groups and bringing them under its control.[42] A fraternalist politics of compensatory domination played a central role in this complex process of courting and containing subaltern groups. In its efforts to consolidate power, the INC began to rely on the logic of fraternalism even while it was decrying its British colonial iteration.

After the successful passage of the Sarda Act, the WIA and the AIWC continued to mobilize for legal reform. Demanding women's expanded access to divorce and their right to inherit and control property, these groups maintained pressure on the INC to push for legal equality. Historian Geraldine Forbes writes that while individual legislators were very supportive of efforts to push for comprehensive legal reform, the INC as a whole proved a "difficult ally" in this struggle.[43] Even though the INC committed itself to just *swaraj* in terms of gender at the 1931 Karachi meeting, for example, it refused the WIA's request to include a statement asserting specifically the "equal right for both men and women in laws relating to marriage, to guardianship of children, inheritance rights and nationality rights" in the "fundamental rights and economic program" the INC produced as a result of the meeting.[44]

After this disheartening refusal, the INC went even further in dashing the leading women's organizations' hopes that it would be a strong supporter of legal rights for women. In March 1931 the INC met with the British government to set the terms of a new governing framework for India at what became known as the Second Round Table Conference. A key question at this conference was how to organize the relationship between the different religious communities so as to avoid Hindu domination and the marginalization of minority groups. The INC presented a "communal settlement" plan designed to address this issue. The plan, which Gandhi presented at the conference, pledged to protect the personal laws of communities.[45] Advocating the inviolability of each religion's personal law was inconsistent with the INC's earlier support of the Sarda Act, which had raised the legal age of marriage across religious communities. The juxtaposition of the INC's support for the Sarda Act and for respecting personal laws suggests that the INC sought to undermine British rule by calling into question the specifically colonial iteration of a fraternalist politics— that is, by interrogating the stakes of the British in women's subordination—yet simultaneously make use of the approach itself in its process of "becoming the raj." It also points to the extent to which minority groups' fears of majority group domination could be appeased by assurances that the system of personal laws would not be disrupted in the transition from colonial to nationalist rule. Although the British were the ones who coercively, if seductively, equated personal law with group autonomy while stripping indigenous groups of political power, the INC supported the system of variable and discriminatory personal laws as a method of courting the consent—or at least attempting to contain the dissent—of minority religious groups to new configurations of nationalist rule.

Feminist groups also attempted to reform Hindu personal laws in particular at this juncture. In 1931 the AIWC unanimously passed a resolution moved by Muthulakshmi Reddi that called upon the organization to press the central legislature to amend Hindu personal law. The AIWC did not mince words in the resolution, which stated that the organization "strongly protests against the existing discrimination in Hindu law against the rights of women; it demands that existing laws should be so amended as to make them just and equitable." In particular, the AIWC made it clear that it supported "complete equality between the sexes in the matter of inheritance and control of property."[46]

The INC's support for Hindu law reform was lackluster at best. Although the AIWC hoped to introduce legislation that would address women's legal position comprehensively, it was pressured by the INC to introduce it piecemeal.[47] In the debates over the measures, detractors argued that such legislation would violate the "sanctity of religious beliefs and practices." Others argued that it would create "havoc in the household." In response to the defeat of these measures, feminist freedom fighter Begum Hamid Ali decried the "utterly unsympathetic attitude" of the men in the legislative assembly who, she argued, were afraid of the personal loss of power and resources that they would suffer if such legislation passed.[48] Another commentator concluded despairingly that "the members of the legislative assembly who are men will not help us in bringing any drastic changes which will benefit women."[49] Ultimately, the legislature did indeed fail to pass measures that would ameliorate women's position with respect to marriage, divorce, and inheritance. The INC's lack of coordinated support for Hindu law reform in the 1930s illustrates its strategy of drawing on the logic of fraternalism not only to gain the support of minority religious groups but to court conservative Hindus as well.

Although they failed to get specific legislation passed, the major Indian women's groups did manage to pressure the British government to set up a committee to investigate Hindu women's property rights. Women's groups were disappointed that no women were included on the committee but nonetheless joined forces to support the committee's efforts. In 1941 the committee, led by B. N. Rau, recommended "comprehensive, fundamental, and substantial modification" of Hindu women's right to property. Two bills emerged from this committee, one dealing with marriage and one with succession. In 1944 the committee was reappointed and was charged with making recommendations for a Hindu code that would be applicable to all communities considered Hindu. As opposed to the all-male first committee, this time the government appointed three women and conducted interviews with women all over the country. The committee's findings leaned strongly in the direction of legal reform. Geraldine Forbes notes that the committee's final report "masterfully blended two views of Hindu society" by arguing that it is "possible to combine the best elements from the ancient Hindu texts with legal principles suitable for contemporary society." The committee report drew out egalitarian interpretations of ancient texts and contemporary practices to serve as the basis of a Hindu law that could support gender equality. Although the report was published in 1946, Parliament postponed its consideration until after independence. While feminist groups were very disappointed by this delay, the report itself demonstrated the compatibility of gender justice with Hindu personal law, an important victory.[50]

While Hindu personal law reforms did not pass in the legislature, Muslim groups were able to reform their personal laws in more gender-equitable ways, albeit through a process that extended and deepened the reach of such law over Indian Muslims. In 1937 the legislature passed the Shariat Act, which consolidated Muslim personal law and further eroded customary law. Pushing strongly for the passage of this legislation, the Jamiat-ul-Ulama-i-Hind and other groups argued that the Shariat Act would give women more rights to inherit and control property, rights ensured by the Koran but eroded, according to these groups, by the influence of local customary laws. This legislation had an ambiguous impact on questions of gender justice. On the one hand, it subjected Muslim women to centralized interpretations of the Shariat and as such limited their legal autonomy and their access to some customary traditions (such as matrilineal traditions) that favored women. On the other hand, feminist scholars have applauded the ways in which a vision of a gender-equitable personal law was central to the debates surrounding the act and to the ways in which the act itself did substantially improve many women's access to property and to divorce. As Azra Asghar Ali puts it, the Shariat Act was "the first ray of sunlight for groups and individuals seeking to change the social as well as political status of Muslim women in India." Furthermore, in 1939 the legislature passed the Dissolution of Muslim Marriages Act of 1939, which gave women greater access to the right of divorce. This legislation was prompted in part by reports that Muslim women were renouncing their faith in order to get a divorce.[51] What is particularly compelling about both the Shariat Act and the Dissolution of Muslim Marriages Act is the extent to which the process of building minority community identity in opposition to a Hindu-dominated polity involved promoting legal equality for women. These acts demonstrate the ways in which, for Muslim groups in the nationalist strug-gle, resisting assimilation also meant working against the enticements of masculinism and challenging the politics of compensatory domination.

The strained relationship of women's groups and the INC during what is known as the "second round" of the struggle for women's suffrage points to another example of the limits of the alliance between women's and nationalist groups, one that marks women's groups' coerced partici-pation in their own political marginalization. While the first struggle for the franchise had been partially successful, it restricted the actual enfran-chisement of women to a female-to-male ratio of 1:20 among eligible voters (who themselves made up only a tiny fraction of the Indian population). Women's groups, in particular the WIA and the AIWC, were determined to expand the franchise to more women and increase women's political repre-sentation. In contrast to the close alliance between nationalist and women's groups during the first round of the suffrage struggle, relations between these groups during the second round were marked by significant strain. Forbes explains that "at the time of the second franchise discussion, the INC expected women's organizations to follow their lead. They left women out of the major discussions, yet counted on complete solidarity. When the women's organizations emerged as a force to be reckoned with, the INC took steps to keep them in check. Women complied but grumbled behind their public documents."[52]

While there were several points of tension between nationalist and wom-en's groups in the second round, one of the major conflicts unfolded over whether women, like minority religions and low-caste groups, should press to increase women's political representation by mechanisms such as allot-ting, or "reserving," a particular number of parliamentary seats for women. The issue of such protective measures, or what became known as "prefer-ential treatment" for minority and other vulnerable groups, was extremely contentious not only for women. Minority religious and low-caste groups argued vociferously for the importance of such measures in preventing upper-caste Hindu dominance in a self-governing India. The INC opposed preferential treatment for minority and other vulnerable groups, arguing that measures such as separate electorates would exacerbate communal tensions and compromise national unity (the INC would eventually have to compromise on this issue). Initially, the major women's groups favored reserved seats and separate electorates for women. Under pressure from the INC leadership, however, the women's groups abandoned their support for these measures and instead advocated communally combined, or "joint," electorates.[53]

In *Specters of Mother India*, Mrinalini Sinha argues that the decision to drop their demands for preferential treatment had negative effects on the direction of the women's movement in India. She explains that the women's groups' support for joint electorates put feminist leadership "in conflict with the demands for separate consideration by religious minorities and by depressed classes in India. . . . The insistence under these circumstances on the representation of women as a unified political bloc became identified with Hindus, as the majority community, and with dominant upper castes who had the most to gain from a unitary conception of the new national polity. . . . Women's collective agency became implicated in an ambiguous political consolidation that provided crucial ideological cover for a reconstituted Hindu, upper-caste, and male polity."[54]

According to Sinha, the women's organizations' support for a unified polity without measures to ensure the political representation of women, religious minority, and low-caste groups—a position adopted in response to pressure from the INC—compromised the relations between women's groups and those religious minority and low-caste groups that favored such measures. Indeed, as Sinha notes, the decision to relinquish the goal of reserved seats "marked a controversial new direction within Indian women's organizations against preferential treatment for any group whatsoever."[55] Women's groups were deeply disappointed when the INC acquiesced in reserving seats for minority and low-caste groups during negotiations with the British. It was difficult to countenance the awarding to others of what the women's groups had been pressured to give up for themselves.

Such compromises on the part of the leadership of women's groups' strained relations within those groups themselves. Muslim women, for example, were forced to choose between the Muslim political parties' support for a differentiated electorate and the women's groups' agreement to a unified polity. These strains disrupted the cross-communal alliance of women from different religious communities that had been so successful in passing legislation such as the Sarda Act and the initial women's suffrage measure.

Furthermore, the attempt to achieve unity by dropping their demands for special treatment made it more difficult for the dominant women's groups to address power relations within their own organizations. The

AIWC, which had previously acknowledged "the need for special provisions for the inclusion of depressed classes" within the organization, began to dismantle those provisions. As Rajkumair Amrit Kaur explained, "We have eliminated the words 'depressed classes.' The word does not exist in our vocabulary." Although Amrit Kaur meant to be inclusive, giving equal importance to demands for gender justice across caste and class in the women's organization, her position and others like it had the effect of stifling debate over issues of caste within the group. Other examples reflect a more straightforward investment in caste or communal privileges. One women's group, for instance, used the discourse of unity to call for the removal of special lower-caste schools.[56]

Sinha observes that relinquishing equal political representation for women had the effect of consolidating upper-caste power and communalism within the women's movement. What is important to emphasize from the perspective of this study is that this consolidation of caste and communal domination within the women's movement came at the price of women's acquiescence in their own political subordination. If the struggle for legal reform was made difficult in part because the INC deployed the politics of compensatory domination, the struggle for electoral reform was complicated by women's groups' own acquiescence in relations of communal, class, and caste domination.

CONCLUSION

The successful movement for Indian independence from British colonial rule illustrates the tremendous power of subordinated groups to challenge inequitable structures of governance by withdrawing their consent. The nationalists achieved this withdrawal in part, as Partha Chatterjee and others have documented, by closing down the "woman question" as a subject of debate with the British. This move was an important signal that the nationalists rejected the terms and conditions of colonial paternalist rule, but it did not end there. In addition to challenging the logic of colonial paternalism, nationalist and feminist groups worked together to oppose policies that legally subordinated and politically marginalized women. In this way they rejected colonial fraternalist policies that offered them control over women as compensation for being ruled by the British themselves. This rejection of both colonial paternalism and colonial fraternalism exposed the emptiness of British discourses of protection and disrupted the conservative alliances upon which the continuation of colonial rule depended.

Examining these moments of resistant convergence of the feminist and nationalist movements suggests the possibility and efficacy of challenging intragroup power relations, and it also points to the possibility of coalitional democratic solidarity. The question of how to link together the struggles of various groups is a pressing one in democratic theory, prompted in part by the expanding array of groups demanding rights and recognition on the basis of race, class, caste, gender, religion, sexual orientation, and ethnicity, among other measures. One of the most important contributions of contemporary feminist and critical race theory is the notion of "intersectionality." Coined by Kimberlé Crenshaw but drawing on work by women of color and third world theorists and activists from the last decades of the twentieth century, intersectionality speaks to the ways that different axes of domination and subordination shape one another. It points as well to the phenomenon in which the interests of the most powerful members of a subordinated group are likely to have the greatest political purchase.[57] The concept of intersectionality has been very fruitfully taken up to expose intragroup power dynamics and illuminate the ways in which the concerns of marginalized subgroups are rendered subordinate to those of the most powerful members of the group. Despite its limits, the struggle for Indian independence represents a very compelling example of a movement that dealt head on with intragroup power relations. The struggle against colonial paternalism and fraternalism generated moments of resistant convergence where both the more and the less powerful members of a subordinated group worked together to challenge domination within the group itself as a critical part of the anticolonial project.

In their influential work on radical democracy, Ernesto LaClau and Chantal Mouffe argue that the democratic reach of any particular struggle can be gauged by the extent to which a group establishes an "equivalence" with other struggles. An equivalence, in this sense, "does not simply establish an 'alliance' between given interests, but modifies the very identity of the forces engaging in that alliance. . . . It is only on this condition that struggles against power become truly democratic, and that the demanding of rights is not carried out on the basis of an individualistic problematic, but in the context of respect for rights to equality of other subordinated groups."[58] What equivalence entails in LaClau and Mouffe's terms is the autonomy of separate struggles so as to ensure that one struggle is not subsumed by another (for example, the subordination of the struggle against sexism to the struggle against capitalism) and an embrace of the proliferation or multiplication of struggles based on identity rather than suspicion of those struggles. The resistant convergence of the nationalist and feminist movements in India suggests that it is essential to resist the politics of compensatory domination—that is, the pressure to dominate the marginalized or less powerful members of one's own subordinated group—if democratic equivalence is to be achieved. Democratic struggle that extends its reach outward to embrace more and more struggles must also involve a simultaneous move inward so that relations within the group are democratically transformed. In the Indian example, the limits of the resistance convergence of the feminist and nationalist movements are as instructive as the successful moments: The democratic potential of the independence movement as a whole was diminished when elite members of otherwise subordinated groups consolidated their own power at the expense of others within their group.

The following chapter explores the ways in which the Constituent Assembly embedded in the constitution the important gains for women and minority groups that the resistant convergence of the nationalist and feminist movements achieved, reconfiguring the exclusionary racial and sexual contracts of Western democracy, but also reasserting control over women as a term of political exchange in the framing of a new, postcolonial social contract. As a document, the new Indian constitution demonstrated both the promise and the limitations of resistant convergence in that it both advanced and compromised the democratic possibilities generated by the struggle for Indian independence.

3

Framing the Postcolonial Social Contract

We are aiming at democracy and nothing less than a democracy. What form of democracy, what shape it might take is another matter. The democracies of the present day, many of them in Europe and elsewhere, have played a great part in the world's progress. Yet it may be doubtful if those democracies may not have to change their shape somewhat before long if they [are] to remain completely democratic. We are not going just to copy, I hope, a certain democratic procedure or an institution of a so-called democratic country. We may improve upon it. . . . We stand for democracy. It will be for this House to determine what shape to give to that democracy, the fullest democracy, I hope.

—*Jawaharlal Nehru, December 13, 1946*

In his opening speech to the Constituent Assembly, the nationalist leader and future prime minister of India Jawaharlal Nehru articulated what he saw as the Assembly's task in its framing of a new constitution for India: the forging of a new, more inclusive model of democracy.[1] Such a democracy would abolish discrimination on the basis of sex, race, religion, and caste, and would not only benefit its own citizenry but stand as a model for the world. In the course of the framers' deliberations, these goals were significantly advanced but also compromised. On the one hand, the Assembly framed a constitution that challenged some of the inequities that had long plagued democratic polities elsewhere—polities democratic in name only. In the transition to independence in India, the framers challenged what Carole Pateman and Charles Mills call, respectively, the sexual and racial contracts underpinning liberal democratic theory and instituted a new kind of social contract, a "postcolonial social contract" designed to foster racial, gender, caste, and minority group equality. On the other hand, despite the explicit constitutional provisions meant to further equality, the framers failed to adequately address the legal subordination of women and the political marginalization of both women and minority groups in the new Indian nation. The postcolonial social contract forged by the Constituent Assembly was thus deeply ambiguous, at once promoting and constraining struggles for caste, minority group, and gender justice in India.

DEMOCRACY'S NEW SIGNATORIES

Although the British touted democracy as an ideal, colonial administrators in India allowed Indians only limited access to democratic representation under the Raj. According to the Indian historian Sumit Sarkar, "the realities of a Raj uncompromisingly white and despotic" were thinly veiled by "an ideology of paternalistic benevolence, occasionally combined with talk of trusteeship and training towards self-government."[2] Even after the colonial government (under immense pressure from the nationalists) began to take steps toward increasing indigenous representation in government, the British jealously guarded the terms and conditions of the political order in India as their racial prerogative. The British government, for example, infuriated nationalists when it sent an all-white delegation, the Simon Commission, to India to consider the appropriate model of government for India in 1928 and designed the Government of India Act of 1935 with little Indian input.[3]

The 1930s and 1940s in India were marked by increasingly vociferous calls for the creation of a Constituent Assembly to frame a constitution for an independent India. In 1934 the INC declared that the only acceptable outcome of negotiations with the British was "a constitution drawn up by a Constituent Assembly elected on the basis of adult franchise." Later, deeply disappointed by the 1935 Government of India Act, under which Britain granted Indians only limited self-government, the INC resolutely reaffirmed that "the Congress stands for a genuine democratic state in India where political power has been transferred to the people, as a whole. Such a state can only come into existence through a Constituent Assembly having the power to determine finally the constitution of the country."[4] By 1945 independence was near; wearied by World War II and faced with growing agitation for freedom in India, the British were ready, in the words of the 1942–45 *satyagraha* (civil disobedience) campaign, to "quit India." The Labour Party in Britain campaigned on the promise to transfer power to India, and soon after taking office declared its support for the creation of an indigenous Constituent Assembly for India. Freedom had been won.

Critical race and feminist theorists have documented the ways in which Western democratic theory has been marked by the exclusion of people of color and women from the social contract. In *The Racial Contract*, for example, Charles Mills argues that people of color are "objects, not subjects of the [social contract] agreement." He explains that the social contract of Western liberal democratic theory is "not a contract between everybody ('we the people'), but between just the people who count, the people who are really people ('we the white people')."[5] In this context, then, calling for an indigenous Constituent Assembly radically disrupted the logic of the racial contract that underlay colonial rule: Indians themselves could and would set forth the framework of a democratic free India. Indeed, although the Assembly was formed while India was still officially a British colony, the INC declared that it would "function in fact, if not in law, as a de facto independent government leading to the full independence to come. The provisional government must have power and authority and responsibility. . . . The members of such a government can only hold themselves responsible to the people and not to any external authority."[6]

When the Assembly met for the first time in December 1946, it made good on this promise by passing a clause declaring its sovereignty. In a *Bombay Chronicle* article entitled "White Man's Burden Gone from 1946!" (January 1, 1947), one commentator noted jubilantly that after the formation of the Assembly, "there can be no return to a state wherein the white men rule the world. . . . Whatever tricks and ruses of champions of the color bar, it is a fact that the oppressed nations have no intention of further accepting the position of political martyrs." Indeed, India's independence from British rule was a momentous instance of what Howard Winant calls the "worldwide rupture of the racial status quo" that occurred at the end of World War II, in which the "customary practices and entrenched institutions of white supremacy" were critically challenged and transformed.[7]

Disrupting the racial contract by rejecting British authority over its proceedings was only the first step in decolonizing democracy for the Constituent Assembly. In *The Racial Contract*, Mills writes that although white-nonwhite relations constitute a tremendously important focus of critique, "it is important not to lose sight of the fact that other subordinate Racial Contracts exist which do not involve white/nonwhite relations."[8] In an independent India, building a truly anticolonial and multicultural democracy would require attention to the mapping of power and privilege along caste, religious, and regional lines, and especially to what were termed "minority and depressed groups" such as Muslims, Sikhs, Avidasis, tribal people, and backward castes. Assembly members were acutely aware of the failures of Western democracies such as the United States to fully include minority and disadvantaged (often termed "backward") groups in the polity and were determined to be more inclusive. In the opening session, delegate N. G. Ranga urged the Constituent Assembly to remember that "in America before the law all the people are equal, but yet you know how depressed are the Negroes of that country. We have to prevent a repetition of that sort of thing in our country." Krishna Sinha echoed this concern, commenting, "it is very necessary that we should set an example by having a state in India which will be a state for the whole of India and at the same time provide safeguards for the fundamental rights of individuals and groups living in this country and for safeguarding the fundamental rights of the minorities."[9]

The sustained struggles against caste and religious domination in the Indian freedom movement oriented the nationalist leadership toward building a democracy that would be both accountable to and reflective of the concerns of minority and deeply disadvantaged groups within the polity. As a result of these struggles, a variety of approaches were pursued to ensure that minority religious groups such as Muslims, Sikhs, Parsis, Christians, and Anglo-Indians and "backward" or disadvantaged groups such as low-caste and tribal groups had representation in the Constituent Assembly, such as reserved seats and proportional representation measures.[10] Further, nationalist leaders often intervened in the provincial selection process to ensure that low-caste, tribal, minority, and women's groups would be represented in the Assembly. Such measures helped lay the groundwork for the participation of marginalized groups in the crafting of the new political order. In his opening speech to the Assembly, for example, Scheduled Caste delegate H. J. Khandekar explained his commitment to bringing the concerns of his community to the Assembly's proceedings: "We are going to frame the constitution of India today. I belong to a community which has been backward and depressed in India for many thousands of years. I am a Harijan and I shall place before you the voice of 90 millions of Harijans in India."[11] If the history of the racial contract rested on the exclusion of marginalized groups from participation in the construction of the terms and conditions of the social contract, many hoped that the inclusion of representatives from minority and oppressed groups in the framing of the Indian constitution would serve to build a more just, inclusive democratic order.

Not everyone was as optimistic as Khandekar, however. Some, such as Jaipal Singh, a member of the Nagpur tribal people, commented that the representation of minority groups in the Assembly was "only a matter of political window dressing." Despite his concerns, however, Singh held out a wary hope that the Assembly would make good on its promises for a new model of multigroup, multicultural democracy. "The house is on trial," he declared, "let us see what happens."[12] In addition, the Muslim League and the Indian National Congress disagreed deeply over the terms of independence. The Muslim League, led by Muhammad Ali Jinnah, feared Hindu dominance in an independent India and demanded that the British set up two constituent assemblies, one for a Muslim state of Pakistan and the other for Hindustan. The INC argued for a single assembly that would design a constitution for a secular state in which both Hindus and Muslims would be united as Indians. The British government sent a cabinet mission to New Delhi in 1946 to try to broker a compromise and proposed a plan in which India would be divided into three regions (one Hindu, one Muslim, and one equally mixed) and the Constituent Assembly would be elected by the provincial legislatures, with seats set aside for the three major communal (religious) groups. Both the League and the Congress cautiously agreed to this plan, and the provincial legislatures elected an Assembly in July 1946. By the end of July, however, Jinnah had accused the INC of acting in bad faith with respect to the cabinet mission plan and declared a boycott of the Assembly. Although several attempts were made to reconcile the League and the Congress (attempts that delayed the convening of the Assembly by six months), they all failed, and the Assembly opened without the League's delegates.

Despite these significant setbacks, the formation of an indigenous Constituent Assembly in India marked a radical disruption of the social contract's racial exclusivity. Similarly, the presence of several women delegates in the Assembly was evidence of an important break with the social contract's gender exclusivity. The groundwork for women's inclusion in the Constituent Assembly was laid both ideologically and institutionally by women's involvement in preindependence Indian politics. In her analysis of women's political participation in India, Susheela Kaushik writes that "their close linking with the national movement helped them acquire the right to political participation, to the franchise and to other constitutional rights. There developed a tacit acceptance of women occupying various positions both in the political and professional spheres. It gave them the space, as well as the power to claim their rights and question its non-compliance."[13]

Reflecting their active participation in the freedom struggle, several key feminist nationalists were chosen to be members of the Constituent Assembly, including Durgabai Deshmukh, Rajkumari Amrit Kaur, Sucheta Kripalani, Hansa Mehta, Sarojini Naidu, Vijaylakshmi Pandit, Begum Aizaz Rasul, and Renuka Ray. In their history of the women's movement in

India, Aparna Basu and Bharati Ray note that the inclusion of women in the Constituent Assembly "was a unique event in the history of the women's movement in the world."[14] Given women's experience in both the legislature and the movement, however, some were surprised that more women were not members of the Constituent Assembly. Jaipal Singh, for example, exclaimed at the opening of the Assembly, "there are too many men in the constituent Assembly. We want more women."[15] Further, although women delegates secured important seats on the Fundamental Rights and the Steering subcommittees, there were no women representatives on the Drafting Committee and the Union Powers Committee, the committees that determined the governing framework and distribution of powers of the new republic.

Even with these limitations, however, women's presence in the Constituent Assembly was tremendously important both symbolically and substantively. Indeed, in her account of her participation in the Constituent Assembly, Renuka Ray remarked that women members "shared equally with the men, perhaps for the first time, the task of formulating ideas in the party meetings and then in the Constituent Assembly itself."[16] The women delegates had tremendous hopes for the realization of gender justice in the democracy that was to be forged by the Assembly. In her opening speech, delegate Hansa Mehta proclaimed, "it will warm the heart of many women to know that free India will mean not only equality of status but also equality of opportunity. What we have asked for is social, political and economic justice. We have asked for that equality which can alone be the basis of mutual respect and understanding without which real cooperation is not possible between man and women."[17] These hopes were to be both realized and dashed in the new social contract forged by the framers.

TOWARD A NEW SOCIAL CONTRACT

When the Constituent Assembly met in 1946, many members looked forward to the opportunity to craft a more inclusive democratic order—a new social contract—that would not only benefit India but serve as a model for other nations as well. In her opening speech, Vijaylakshmi Pandit predicted that "in an independent India the fullest social, economic, and cultural justice to individuals and groups will be conceded and through our design for living, we shall be helping other nations to decide the pattern of their own lives." Further, in contrast to heavy-handed British wielding of sovereignty, the Assembly leadership hoped that the authority of the new Indian state would be based, in the words of Sardar Patel, on "a consent performance, not a command performance."[18]

Among the first acts of the Constituent Assembly was the establishment of an electorate based on universal adult suffrage. In making this decision, the Assembly enfranchised millions of Indians and removed the gender, tax, education, and property qualifications to voting specified in the 1935 Government of India Act. In doing so, the Assembly made good on the nationalist promise that independence would bring such change.[19] According to Zoya Hasan, "the establishment of democracy and universal adult suffrage in a hierarchical society characterized by unprecedented social inequality, deprivation, and oppression was undoubtedly a revolutionary principle, a bold experiment in political affairs, perhaps the most significant in any country."[20]

In addition to universal adult suffrage, the Assembly confirmed as a central objective of the new polity that "adequate safeguards shall be provided for minorities, backward and tribal areas, and depressed and other backward classes." In the initial draft of the constitution, these safeguards included provisions for reserved seats in the legislatures for minority groups, quotas in government employment, and administrative mechanisms to ensure the protection of minority rights.[21] Further, on the recommendation of the Fundamental Rights Subcommittee, the Assembly passed justiciable (legally enforceable) fundamental rights measures that guaranteed equality among the sexes; barred state discrimination on the basis of sex, race, religion, and caste; forbade exclusionary employment or occupational practices on the basis of sex, race, religion, or caste; abolished untouchability; and provided for equality of opportunity and opened up all public offices to women. By lifting formal restrictions to public political life for women and minorities and explicitly recognizing the need to address questions of gender, caste, and minority group equality, the framers challenged the exclusions that had long plagued liberal democratic state formations as well as indigenous hierarchies that were bolstered and consolidated by the British. Reflecting upon these measures, delegate H. V. Pataskar commented that "people of India should feel convinced that the interests of every Indian, irrespective of caste, creed, religion, sex, and social and economic status, will be safeguarded in the future constitution which we propose to frame." Echoing this sentiment, delegate Begum Aizaz Rasul commented, "as a woman, I have very great satisfaction in the fact that no discrimination will be made on account of sex. It is in the fitness of things that such a provision should have been made in the draft constitution and I am sure women can look forward to equality of opportunity under the new constitution."[22]

Having established these important measures toward gender, caste, and minority group justice as fundamental to the polity, the framers next turned to the issue of what kind of state—centralized or decentralized—a free India was to be. This was an extremely contentious question, especially given the tensions between the INC and the Muslim League over the terms and conditions of centralized governance. As mentioned above, however, the Muslim League became distrustful of the INC's commitment to the compromise governance framework, in which the central legislature would have very limited jurisdiction, and boycotted the Assembly. In 1947, unable to find a solution, the British partitioned India into two independent states, India and Pakistan. In addition to instigating a massive demographic shift that left the Muslims remaining in India with deeply attenuated political power, partition and partition-related violence formed the backdrop of the Constituent Assembly's proceedings and shaped the framers' approaches to issues of governance, national unity, and minority rights.

From another perspective, Mahatma Gandhi was also an opponent of a strong centralized state, arguing that such a model would undermine the goal of *swaraj* (self-rule) as well as abandon India's own history of decentralized, village-level governance. When asked, in late July 1946, to give a picture of the "kind of independence" that he imagined for India, he replied, "Independence must begin at the bottom. Thus every village will be a republic of *panchayat* [village council] having full powers. . . . In this structure, composed of innumerable villages, there will be ever-widening, never-ascending circles." Gandhi worried, however, that the Constituent Assembly would choose a model of governance based on colonial administrative structures; such a government, he argued, would amount to "English rule without the English, keeping the tiger's nature without the tiger." He noted that although "the Constituent Assembly has all the possibilities for the realization of my picture . . . I cannot hope for much. . . . I know that many would have India become a first-class military power and wish for India to have a strong center and build the whole structure round it."[23]

After partition made moot the compromise governance framework that stipulated a weak central government, the Assembly's leadership endorsed a centralized governance framework, and the constitution proposed by the Drafting Committee was largely drawn, as Gandhi had feared, from the British model of colonial administration, in particular the 1935 Government of India Act. The Assembly was convinced that a decentralized framework of governance would leave the newly independent India weak in the face of potential adversaries and unable effectively to address poverty and internal strife. For Nehru and other Assembly leaders, the magnitude of the problems that India faced—partition-related communal violence, famine, external threats—required a state strong enough to engineer a social revolution. Nehru, for one, argued that "it would be injurious to the interests of the country to provide for a weak central authority which would be incapable of ensuring peace, of coordinating vital matters of common concern and of speaking effectively for the country in the international sphere." Speaking on behalf of the Drafting Committee, Nehru announced that "now that partition is a settled fact, we are unanimously of the view that the soundest framework for our constitution is a federation, with a strong center."[24] In the words of Assembly delegate K. M. Munshi, after partition, the Assembly was "free to form a federation of our choice, a federation with a center as strong as we can make it."[25]

The political scientist Paul Brass notes that in addition to being motivated by hope and inspiration for a more inclusive democracy, the framers' deliberations were also animated by a deep fear of disorder. The decision to build a political order based on a strong centralized state was in part a consequence of that fear. After independence, Brass notes, "the fear of disorder and the desire for a strong central government, termed a 'strong Centre' in Indian parlance, went together." Brass suggests that this politics of order has had damaging consequences: "This focus on combating disorder and maintaining order has been part of a whole range of ideologies, policies, non-policies and practices that have been sustaining not just 'order' in the abstract, but a particular social and economic order, particular patterns of dominance and subordination, and particular relations of power. For this fear of disorder has preoccupied the minds of India's dominant upper caste and upper class political, social, and economic elites for the past 50 years. It is a fear not just of disunity, disintegration, decay, and violence, but a fear of the people, of the dangers to their own status and well-being if the poor and the low castes should at last begin to organize and to challenge their dominance."[26]

The tension between hope for an inclusive, egalitarian democracy and fear of disorder was also reflected in the framers' decisions on the relationship between national unity and the rights of minority groups. While committed to a pluralist polity, the framers were at the same time deeply worried about the prospect of division and sectarianism in postpartition India. The challenge was thus both to ensure the protection of minority group rights and to build a unified state. In response to this challenge, the framers attempted to build a homogenous, secular public sphere, while simultaneously enabling a heterogeneous private sphere that would allow for group difference and autonomy. Strategic use of a rhetoric of fraternity maintained a precarious balance between the two spheres.

The first moves toward a homogenous public sphere occurred after partition, when, in what Rochana Bajpai calls a "remarkable reversal," Assembly members overturned measures they had passed earlier to safeguard the political inclusion of religious minority groups, such as reserved seats and separate electorates, while leaving them in place for low castes and tribal groups.[27] These arguments often drew upon the language of fraternal kinship to describe the relationship between groups in India, in particular between Hindus and Muslims. Assembly member Biswanth Das, for example, urged his fellow Assembly members to remember that "my Muslim brothers are blood of my blood and bone of my bones. They are mine and I belong to them and they belong to me."[28] Bajpai notes that in these debates the majority Hindus cast themselves in the role of the "responsible, easy-going, benevolent and self-sacrificing elder brother, indulgent, protective, and accommodating of even the excessive and unreasonable demands of his younger and weaker brothers, the minorities."[29] Those who opposed reversing the measures—mostly members of minority group—argued that ensuring minority group representation through political safeguards would be compatible with a secular, democratic framework and would enhance rather than disrupt fraternal relations. "No danger or harm can follow," argued delegate Naziruddin Ahmad, "if the elder brother listens to the grievances of the younger brother."[30] Despite these pleas, those advocating a homogenous political sphere prevailed, and the Hindu-dominated Constituent Assembly overturned the protective measures it had passed earlier to ensure the robust inclusion of minority groups in the political sphere.

In invoking the concept of fraternity in these debates, Assembly members appealed to an ideal of fraternity based not only on shared kinship among groups but also on the idea of masculinist solidarity. For example, when the Assembly voted to abolish the system of separate electorates for minority groups, delegate Pattabhi Sitaramayya explained, "We are entering upon a new period in the development of our country. . . . When new joint electorates are formed . . . I can go to Janab Mahboob Ali Beg's [a fellow Muslim Assembly member] house and address his mother and he may come to my house and address my wife, we can invite each other to dinner, we can exchange the best of cordialities in life and become brothers once again."[31] Sitaramayya's invocation of a fraternalism grounded in gestures toward each other's wives and mothers suggests the close linkages between moves toward an allegedly homogenous political sphere and the preservation of gender roles and masculinist authority in the home. It is in each other's homes, Sitaramayya suggests, that he and his fellow Assembly member can best recognize each other as brothers. The home, of course, is not a neutral place; indeed, it was in the home that masculinist authority was legally entrenched under British colonial rule through the system of personal laws specific to different religious groups in India—laws that discriminated against women in such matters as marriage, divorce, and inheritance. As much as legal gender discrimination contradicted the framers' pledge of gender equality, the Assembly's debates over attempts to abolish, challenge, or modify this system of personal law point to the extent to which fraternal solidarity depended on the preservation of control over women in the family.

Delegates made several attempts to overturn or reform the system of personal laws that had been established by the British. The first such attempt originated in the Fundamental Rights Subcommittee, when Hansa Mehta, Rajkumari Amrit Kaur, B. R. Ambedkar, and Minoo Masani recommended that separate personal laws be eliminated and a uniform civil code that would be progressive with respect to caste and gender rights and applicable to all communities be instituted as a fundamental right.[32] The measure was defeated in the subcommittee in a 5–4 vote, the majority arguing that enacting such a provision would exceed the authority of the committee.[33] Mehta, Kaur, Ambedkar, and Masani reluctantly agreed to a compromise in which the provision for a uniform civil code was included in a list of "directive principles" that would be legally unenforceable but would guide the legislators of the new state toward more just social arrangements.

Having failed to institute a uniform civil code, proponents of personal law reform next attempted to use the constitution's equality clause to challenge inequities within the legal system. Renuka Ray tried to persuade her fellow Assembly members that it should be made clear that constitutional provisions for gender equality would apply to each community's personal laws:

> With regard to fundamental rights, equal rights have been prescribed. Quite rightly, it has been laid down that the State shall not discriminate against any citizen on grounds of religion, race or sex. But in view of conditions in this country . . . I think it is necessary to have an explicit provision that social laws of marriage and inheritance of the different communities shall not also have any disabilities attached to them on grounds of caste or sex. It is of course true that the right of equality includes this [idea] but there may be different interpretations and much confusion and I therefore appeal to the House to have a proviso to explain this.[34]

Ray's appeal, like the earlier attempt in the Fundamental Rights Subcommittee, was rebuffed.

Proponents of personal law reform also attempted to pass reforms that would ameliorate caste and gender subordination within Hindu personal law in particular. Based largely on the Rau Committee report, the Hindu Code Bill would have made sweeping changes in the laws governing marriage and inheritance. Ramachandra Guha explains that Hindu Code Bill had two main purposes: "first, to elevate the rights and status of Hindu women; second, to do away with the disparities and divisions of caste." Among other measures promoting caste and gender equity, the Hindu Code Bill would have abolished caste restrictions on marriage and adoption, such that "all marriages between Hindus would have the same sacramental as well as legal status, regardless of the castes to which the spouses belonged [and] inter-caste marriage could be solemnized in accordance with the customs and rites of either party." The bill would also have outlawed polygamy and increased women's inheritance rights.[35]

When presented to the Assembly in 1949, however, the bill faced immense opposition. As Assembly member Sucheta Kripalani observed, "Ever since we had a sovereign legislature, no piece of legislation has given rise to greater excitement and controversy than this Hindu Code Bill." In his argument against the bill, Pandit Lakshmi Kanta Maitra claimed that the measure would "give rise to bitterness, disunion, and discord in our families leading to the disintegration of society. . . . It will completely unsettle a well settled order of things."[36] After weeks of conflict and filibustering, Assembly leaders decided to withdraw the bill from consideration. By relegating the uniform civil code to a nonjusticiable directive principle and failing to challenge the caste and gender inequities embedded in the personal laws themselves, the framers of the constitution reinforced caste hierarchy and control over women as crucial elements of fraternity in the new Indian polity.

The proposals to abolish or reform the system of personal laws caused a tremendous uproar in the Assembly. While supporters of maintaining protective legislation for group representation couched their arguments in the language of fraternity, speeches opposing a uniform civil code tended to emphasize that such a code would deeply disrupt harmonious fraternal relations in the new polity. In arguing against the interference of the new Indian state in different communities' personal laws, for example, Assembly member Mohammad Ismail threatened that any interference in matters of marriage and succession would engender "disharmony," but he reassured the Assembly that "if people are allowed to follow their own personal law there will be no discontent or dissatisfaction."[37] Delegate Pocker

Bahadur argued that noninterference had been the "secret of success" in British rule in India:

> The House will note that one of the reasons why the Britisher, hav-ing conquered the country, has been able to carry on the administra-tion of this country for the last 150 years and over was that he gave a guarantee of following their own personal laws to each of the various communities in the country. This is one of the secrets of success and the basis of the administration of justice on which even the foreign rule was based. . . . In saying this, I am voicing forth the feeling of ever so many sections in this country who feel that it would really be tyrannous to interfere with the religious practices, and the religious laws, by which they are governed now.[38]

Given that the religious laws in question consolidated masculinist authority in the family, Bahadur articulated a particularly stark portrayal of the fraternal bargain underpinning colonial rule: Control over women was offered in exchange for acquiescence in British rule. In Bahadur's view, threats to masculinist authority would have a destabilizing effect; indeed, if the Constituent Assembly withdrew the fraternal bargain set in place by the British, he suggested, men might withdraw their obedience to the state.

COMPARING THE CONTRACTS

Although the preamble to the new constitution had been passed by the Assembly in 1946, in May 1948 the Drafting Committee revisited the ques-tion of the preamble, replacing the clauses that had provided for autonomous provinces with an appeal to "fraternity, assuring the dignity of the individual and the unity of the nation."[39] Constituent Assembly historian Panchanand Misra wrote that since the Drafting Committee believed that the "partition and disintegrating forces necessitated the establishment of a strong central government . . . the committee had felt that there was a great need for fra-ternal concord and goodwill in India and that this particular aim of the new constitution should be emphasized by special mention in the preamble."[40] In *The Sexual Contract*, Pateman urges her readers to pay close attention to the deployment of the rhetoric of fraternity in democratic discourses. For Pate-man, fraternity is an underacknowledged component of the resolution of the democratic authority problematic in social contract theory. In her account

of the sexual contract that underlies Western political theory, a central reason why men who were ostensibly equals—political brothers—agreed to be
governed was so as to preserve and enhance their power over women. In
part to resolve the contradiction between democracy's ethos of equality and
assertions of masculine power, Pateman argues, Western political theorists
separated the public and private spheres: The public sphere would be the
arena in which principles of equality and freedom would operate, and in
the private sphere relations of domination and subordination would legitimately prevail. Men could move freely between both spheres, but women
were excluded from the public sphere and dominated the private sphere.[41]
In *The Racial Contract,* Mills argues that the brotherhood Pateman describes
is severely circumscribed by race. The racial contract, Mills claims, generates
a political order that legitimates and consolidates white supremacy and is
geared toward the exploitation of the land and labor of people of color.

In contrast to the racialized and gendered fraternities of Western democracy, however, the framers of the Indian constitution were committed to the
principle, forged in the freedom struggle, that national liberation would
mean emancipation for women, low-caste, and minority religious groups
as well. Even the most socially conservative members of the Assembly
asserted their support for universal suffrage, and there was very little dissent in the debate over the passage of the fundamental rights clauses that
called for gender, racial, religious, and caste equality in the public sphere.
By orienting the polity toward justice for women, the disadvantaged, and
minority groups, the framers challenged the exclusions of democracy's
social contract and established new frameworks of gender and racial governance in what, in critical contract terms, could be called a "postcolonial
social contract." Comparing and contrasting the gendered and racialized
frameworks articulated in the postcolonial social contract with Pateman's
description of the sexual contract and Mills's account of the racial contract reveals the ways in which the framing of the Indian constitution both
advanced and compromised the struggle for a more egalitarian democracy.

According to Pateman, the story of the sexual contract in Western liberal democratic theory is "a story of women's subjection."[42] By contrast,
the story of the postcolonial sexual contract embedded in the postcolonial
social contract is a story at once of women's emancipation and of their subjection. Indeed, in the process of forging the new Indian polity, the framers
reconfigured the sexual contract by formally providing for women's participation in the public sphere; but they also maintained men's dominance in
the family by preserving the system of personal laws developed under the
British. This contradictory resolution of the "woman question" underlies

the postcolonial sexual contract in India. Under its terms, women were no longer restricted from entering, and indeed were guaranteed equality in, the public sphere. This formal recognition of equality represents an important step toward a more egalitarian model of democracy. In its landmark 1974 report *Towards Equality*, for example, the Committee on the Status of Women in India paid tribute to the framers' inclusion of political equality for women in the constitution, writing that their "recognition of political equality of women was a radical departure not only in India but also in the context of the political evolution of even the most advanced countries of that date." Such a constitutional endorsement of women's political rights, the committee explained, meant that they could assert the importance of women's political equality "as a settled fact, for which no discussion was necessary."[43] This achievement can be contrasted to the long and ultimately unsuccessful struggle for passage of the Equal Rights Amendment in the United States. Indeed, the notion of gender equality as a fundamental right codified in the constitution has remained available to feminists and other progressive activists in India who have called upon this heritage to contest discriminatory personal laws and women's political marginalization, and thus to destabilize the postcolonial social contract. However, by maintaining personal laws that discriminated against women in terms of property ownership, inheritance, marriage, and divorce, the Assembly perpetuated the legal subordination of women in the family in the postcolonial polity. Agreeing to a compromise that created a uniform civil code as a nonbinding directive principle, even nationalist leaders firmly committed to women's emancipation sanctioned the continuation of discriminatory laws.

When compared to the racial contract that Mills describes, the postcolonial racial contract advanced notions of racial and minority group equality by radically disrupting the exclusionary logic of colonial rule, which held that people of color were either not entitled to or not ready for democratic self-rule. Furthermore, by formally barring discrimination based on caste, race, ethnicity, or religion, the framers laid the groundwork for a democracy that addressed indigenous racialized hierarchies as well. As Zoya Hasan notes, India was "one of the few countries in the post-colonial world that took up the challenge of building an inclusive democracy in a highly diverse, multicultural, multilingual, and multi-religious society."[44] In addressing hierarchies of caste, tribe, and religion, the framers of the constitution developed two contrasting but interacting approaches, one for minority religious groups and one for low-caste groups, each shaped by the postindependence political context and each advancing and compromising the goals of equality and social justice in different ways.

For minority religious groups, the framers instituted measures that would protect differential group identity formation. These measures included constitutional guarantees of freedom of religion, the freedom to establish religious educational institutions, and legal pluralism. Rajeev Bhargava explains that the framers attempted in this way to "contain discrimination and rectify perception of disadvantage among minorities . . . by granting groups a degree of control over their affairs by different rights of self-government, including the rights to express cultural particularity."[45] Particularly important among these measures was the recognition of different communities' personal laws, for such recognition protected a group's jurisdictional autonomy.

While these provisions for legal pluralism and religious freedom ensured a degree of autonomy over group cultural and religious life, the framers' decision to withdraw measures that would have ensured the political strength of minority groups (such as reserved seats and communal electorates), in favor of a homogenous political sphere, cemented majority group domination in national political life. Hasan suggests that in addressing questions of justice for minority groups, the framers made a "trade-off" between cultural recognition and political representation. One consequence of that trade-off, she explains, is that debates about "minorities and their rights were cut off from the discourse of disadvantage and social justice" and located in the realm of cultural diversity. As a result, "minority rights were often conceived in the language of respect and protection, but social and economic rights were missing from this framework."[46]

For minority religious groups, then, the postcolonial racial contract was marked by autonomy or group sovereignty in the spheres of the family and religion, and by marginalization in the national political sphere. This formulation of the postcolonial racial contract was closely intertwined with the postcolonial sexual contract: Given that minority group personal laws discriminated against women, control over women functions in this framework as a marker of group sovereignty.

In addressing the question of how to work toward justice and equality for low-caste and tribal groups, the framers took a different approach, establishing a system of reservations to facilitate their participation in processes of national decision making. The Constituent Assembly also recommended affirmative action measures to ensure the castes and tribes access to educational institutions and state employment. Finally, the framers abolished untouchability and outlawed discrimination in public places on the basis of caste. Hasan explains that the adoption of these measures "marked a turning point in India's political history with regard to the constitutional design and state policies of inclusion and affirmative action for Scheduled Castes, Scheduled Tribes, and backward classes more generally," and provided mechanisms for these groups and their supporters to work against entrenched social and economic disadvantages.[47]

For low-caste and tribal groups, then, the configuration of the postcolonial racial contract was marked by the legal abolition of caste discrimination and the provision of measures for substantive inclusion in the political sphere. While these measures represented substantial advances in the struggle for caste and tribal justice, they were nonetheless limited. For one thing, the framers rejected a more comprehensive reform of caste hierarchy that would have abolished "any privilege or disability arising out of rank, birth, person, family, religions, or religious usage and custom."[48] In addition, they explicitly linked the notion of "backwardness" to the Hindu caste system rather than to a more capacious understanding of social disadvantage more generally, thus excluding other minority religious groups from the avenues of redress and inclusion that the constitution provided for low-caste and tribal groups.

Despite the ways in which the Assembly used religion to circumscribe social redress on the basis of caste, the significant success of these measures for the political inclusion of castes in postcolonial India has inspired women and minority groups to press for such measures as well. Indeed, the variegated nature of the framers' approach to caste, gender, and minority group justice enables groups to compare and contrast approaches that are particularly efficacious in challenging domination and marginalization. Further, when compared to the justificatory rhetoric of both the racial and the sexual contracts, these iterations of the postcolonial racial and sexual contracts differ in an important way: They leave uncovered the contradictions that the racial and sexual contracts hide. In the sexual contract that Pateman describes, for example, the paradox of freedom for men and subordination for women in a supposedly egalitarian democratic order is submerged by insulating the public sphere from women's participation and by portraying women as irrational and in need of protection. Similarly, according to the rhetoric of the racial contract that Mills describes, the contradiction between the democratic ethos of equality and the reality of the exclusion and subordination of people of color was concealed by casting them as either unfit or unready for self-rule and by marginalizing their participation in political life. Under the postcolonial social contract, however, because gender, race, religious, caste, and ethnic equality are enshrined as constitutional principles, the contradiction between the democratic ethos of equality and the reality of subordination and political marginalization of these groups is exposed, leaving the contract itself more open to challenge.

In the chapters that follow, I explore challenges to the postcolonial social contract in present-day Indian politics. I argue that if these challenges are to be successful, it is important to disrupt the logic that keeps struggles for minority group, gender, and caste justice in opposition to one another. If these struggles can be linked, I suggest, then challenges to women's legal subordination and efforts to enhance women's participation in electoral politics have the potential to destabilize the postcolonial social contract in ways that open the door for democratic configurations more conducive to groups that have been denied the promises of decolonization.

4

Challenging Political Marginalization:
The Women's Reservation Bill

In the closing days of the Constituent Assembly, delegate Rohini Kumar Chaudhuri proposed a provision to the constitution that would ensure "protection from women," arguing that this was necessary because "in every sphere of life they [women] are now trying to elbow us out. In the offices, in the legislatures, in the embassies, in everything they try to elbow us out. . . . If the feelings of man are such that he should push them forward I would very much regret it. . . . It is the foolish man who wishes to give them votes and send them to the legislatures and thus create troubles like the trouble which they have created in the matter of the Hindu code." Although the Assembly rejected his provision, Chaudhuri's comments point to the vulnerability of masculinist power under the terms and conditions of the postcolonial social contract: Women's access to the public sphere potentially gave them the power to challenge their legal subordination within the family. Indeed, anxiety over fraternal maintenance of power resurfaced again in the final session of the Constituent Assembly, when delegate B. Das noted that "women are about 50 percent of the population," adding, "I do not want that they should give battle at the time of the next elections on this ground. I do not want a pitched battle between Man and Woman." Assembly speaker and future president of India Rajendra Prasad reassured Das that this would not happen, remarking, "we could not compel any electorate to send in women."[1]

Far from forcing the electorate to choose women candidates, the Congress listed only eighteen women as contestants in the 1952 elections.[2] Madhu Kishwar and others note that, after independence, "women were pushed out of leadership positions to function on the margins, at best relegated to the domain of social work at the local level."[3] Despite constitutional measures guaranteeing women the fundamental right of access and equality in the public sphere, women were severely underrepresented in India's legislative bodies after independence. With women's formal political equality a stark contradiction to the blatantly discriminatory personal laws, their political marginalization in the new Indian polity served in part to submerge the contradictions of the postcolonial social contract.

Indian feminist groups and others, however, have consistently resisted this marginalization. This chapter examines the debate over one such effort to combat women's political marginalization, the Women's Reservation Bill. Passed by the Rajya Sabha in 2010, after fourteen years of rancorous parliamentary debate, this bill would amend the constitution to mandate 33 percent representation for women in the Indian parliament.[4]

RESERVATIONS FOR WOMEN: CALLING THE QUESTION

On December 9, 1996, fifty years after the Constituent Assembly met for the first time, Geeta Mukherjee urged her fellow legislators to pass legislation providing for the allotment of 33 percent of the seats in Parliament for women. "Today is the fiftieth anniversary of the first sitting of the Constituent Assembly," she explained. "This is one of the subjects which we could take up in honor of this occasion. . . . I join all my friends in demanding that the bill be passed without delay."[5] The Women's Reservation Bill, as the legislation became known, followed on the heels of similar legislation, passed in 1993, that established 33 percent representation for women in the village-level legislative bodies (*panchayats*).[6] The subject of fierce and sometimes violent debate, the bill was proposed for consideration several times between its first introduction in 1996 and its passage by the Rajya Sabha in 2010.[7]

The issue of reserving a certain percentage of parliamentary seats for women was hotly debated even before independence. One milestone in long struggle toward this end came with the publication, in 1974, of the groundbreaking government report *Towards Equality: Report of the Committee on the Status of Women in India*. The Indian Ministry of Education and Social Welfare commissioned this report to investigate the status of women after independence, in anticipation of the United Nations' International Women's Year in 1975. Led by Dr. Phulrenu Guha, a veteran of the freedom struggle, the ten-member committee of women activists, academics, and politicians toured the country and interviewed more than five hundred women in each Indian state.[8]

Towards Equality found that despite the constitution's guarantees of gender equality, "there has been some regression from the normative attitudes developed during the freedom movement." The report found that although women had made good strides in entering professions, they still were woefully underrepresented in the legislatures, their representation in Parliament fluctuating between 4 and 8 percent. Given these statistics and the evidence gathered on its tour of the country, the committee concluded that "the right to political equality has not enabled women to play their roles as partners and constituents in the political process."[9]

The committee attributed the "declining trend in the number of women legislators" primarily to the reluctance of male-dominated political parties to sponsor women candidates. According to the report, the parties paid "lip service to the cause of women's progress" but allowed only "a few women in the legislative and executive wings of government." Furthermore, "the minority and dependent status" of women who did manage to get elected presented "serious obstacles to their acting as spokesmen for women's rights and opportunities."[10] Although the committee had not initially included a question about reserving seats for women in its survey, it acknowledged that several women's groups across the country urged committee members to press for reserved seats for women on the local, state, and national levels so as to remedy women's political marginalization. According to these groups, affirmative action in the political sphere was needed in order to push political parties to sponsor women candidates for office.

Towards Equality officially recommended allotting seats for women only at the local level (in village *panchayats* and municipal bodies), however, arguing that reservations on the state or national level would be too "major [a] change in our political structure." The report maintained that imposing such a reform at the state or national level could isolate women from men, when the history of the movement demonstrated that "the women's cause in India has always been championed by all progressive elements, men as well as women." Such a major change could also precipitate demands from other groups for guaranteed parliamentary seats, the report warned, and thus "threaten national integration." The issue of reserved seats, however, was tremendously contentious within the committee itself, and three members opposed the decision to limit reservations for women to local institutions. Two of these dissenters, Lotika Sarkar and Vina Mazumdar, suggested that the low percentage of women elected to Parliament was a "sufficient indicator of the reluctance of our society to accept the principle of equal representation for women." Given this societal reluctance, they argued, ensuring a baseline of women's political representation through reservation could be an effective way to "achieve the desired goals" of gender equality called for in the constitution.[11]

In the 1980s, women legislators like Margaret Alva, the minister for women at the time, worked to translate the committee's recommendations into policy. In 1992 Parliament passed the seventy-first and seventy-second amendments to the constitution, known as the *panchayati raj* bills, which enhanced the power of the *panchayats* as bodies of governance and provided for 33 percent representation for women. For Alva and her allies, the push for reserved seats for women in the *panchayats* was meant as a stepping stone for the same in both houses of Parliament. "From the beginning," Alva explains, "the intention was to go right up to Parliament. That was our demand but there was quite a lot of opposition at that time. So it was decided that we should start with the Panchayati Raj amendments and move up later."[12]

In September 1996 Alva introduced what was then the Eighty-First Amendment to the Constitution Bill, which called for the government to set aside 33 percent of the seats in the Lok Sabha and the state legislatures for women representatives. The amendment would achieve this goal by reserving certain constituencies, determined by a lottery system that would rotate in each election, for women candidates. The amendment would also reserve 33 percent of the seats within the quota of seats reserved for low-caste and tribal groups, also known as Scheduled Castes (SCs) and Scheduled Tribes (STs), for women of those communities. At that time, women held 6 percent of the seats in the Lok Sabha; Madhu Kishwar noted that "by reserving one-third of the seats in legislatures, India will be ensuring a quantum leap. . . . The very presence of 181 women in the Lok Sabha will make them much more visible, a drastic difference from their miniscule presence today."[13] The measure's potential to bring about a profound shift in social and political relations was not lost on either the bill's supporters or its opponents; indeed, the specter of women's participation in politics on a large scale provoked heated debates animated by hopes and anxieties surrounding the implications of such a change for politics, for the family, and for the stability and unity of the Indian state.

REPRESENTING WOMEN: CONCERNS AND RESPONSES

In her essay "Can the Subaltern Speak?" Gayatri Spivak distinguishes between two "related but irreducibly discontinuous" senses of representation: representation as "speaking about," in writing ("re-presentation"), and representation as "speaking for" or "stepping in someone's place," in politics. She envisions a practice that would self-consciously "attend to this double session of representations," explaining that acts of representation always include moments of re-presentation. Whereas Spivak highlights the ways in which political representation can illuminate the politics of re-presentation and vice versa, Rajeswari Sunder Rajan takes this relationship one step further, arguing that the critiques of each sense of representation must be brought to bear upon each other. She notes that while critiques of representation in writing have been a rich site for the theorization of subject formation in feminist theory, these critiques have not been fully taken up in feminist theorizations of the sense of representation "that democratic politics enforces—where the one stands for and protects the interests of the many in a nation's legislative and executive bodies."[14] While acknowledging that the two senses of the word do not describe the same phenomenon, Rajan argues that they can be read analogically, suggesting that the problematic of one can be explored via the problematic of the other.

I analyze below the debates on the Women's Reservation Bill using an analogical approach that draws upon the one that Rajan recommends. In particular, I employ Kamala Visweswaran's notion of "failure" as an analytical tool that can uncover the limits of representation as "speaking about" others in an ethnographic vein and also point to the limits of representation as "speaking for" others in the political sense of the word. Visweswaran uses the notion of failure to critically interrogate her own representative practice as an ethnographer. In response to a "failed" interview, for example, she writes that "failure signals a project that may no longer be attempted, or at least not on the same terms." In the parliamentary debates over the Women's Reservation Bill, the specter of failure was often invoked: Both supporters and opponents of the bill worried about women's potential failure to serve as competent legislators, to remain uncorrupted by politics, and to adequately represent the diversity of Indian women. I read the specter of these failures in the vein recommended by Visweswaran: as indicators that the terms of political engagement must be shifted and that political power relations must no longer remain the same.[15]

The debates over the Women's Reservation Bill reveal deep anxieties regarding women's willingness and ability to serve as representatives and the possibility that they might fail in this role. Indeed, one common objection of opponents was that there would not be enough women to fill the allotted seats if the bill passed. Critics argued that it would be exceedingly difficult to "find women who will seek election in the rural areas. . . . They are too conservative, mostly living in purdah."[16] Even if enough women could be found to run for office, the bill's detractors claimed, they would not be able perform the duties required of them as parliamentarians. MP Pramila Dandavate noted that opponents of the bill "asked so many questions" about women's ability to participate in electoral politics: "Will she open her mouth? Will she be articulate? Will she understand? Do women have the time? Where will they come from? How will they come? They are so illiterate!" "Such questions," exclaimed Dandavate scornfully, when "there are so many *mauni babas* [meditative saints] in the Parliament who never open their mouths!"[17]

In response to these criticisms, the bill's supporters pointed to women's pivotal involvement in the freedom struggle. Margaret Alva reminded her fellow legislators in Parliament that the scarcity of women legislators in postindependence India could not be blamed on a shortage of politically involved women but lay squarely on the failure of male party leaders to back them for seats. "Think back to 1952—the first general elections," said Alva. "The percentage of women elected to the first Lok Sabha was only 4.4. Are we to believe that among the stalwart freedom fighters of our country there was such a dearth of capable women that they could not put up more candidates and get them in Parliament?"[18] Alva and other backers of the bill maintained that when given the opportunity, women would become enthusiastically involved in politics. On the local level, as Dandavate explained, "they have even exceeded the quota; for example, in Karnataka, women constitute forty-seven per cent of the elected panchayat members."[19]

Critics of the bill were also concerned about the level of autonomy women would be able to exercise as legislators, given their subordination in the home, a concern shared by some feminist activists, such as Madhu Kishwar.[20] Instead of creating a set of women representatives attuned and responsive to the needs and concerns of women, some argued that reservations for women would lead to "biwi-beti brigades" (wife-and-daughter brigades) in which female politicians would represent their male relatives' interests. MP Uma Bharti explained that "in many rural areas the husband of an elected woman automatically begins to act as if he is a member of the panchayat. He even manages to sit alongside her, and he keeps signaling to her what he wants her to do. Everyone knows what is going on. . . . When people have proposals they even go to the extent of contacting the husband directly."[21] In defense of the bill, others argued that women's experience in politics would transform the household power relations underlying the "biwi-beti" dynamic. Dandavate maintained that "a woman whose decision has so much importance outside is gradually given recognition even within her family. Her position in the family changes due to her position outside. It is not the other way around." Dandavate explained that "in the beginning, even in the rural areas, women listen to their husbands. But slowly they realize that their own opinion and their own power matters, and they begin to assert it."[22] From this point of view, women's enhanced political representation would shift power relations in the family, thus undermining male dominance in the home.

Another line of argument focused on the threat that women representatives might pose to men's electoral power. The possibility of a gendered shift in representation, Alva argued, alarmed and frightened the bill's detractors. "The greatest fear among male [opponents to the bill is] that they will lose their seats," she said in an interview.[23] Even Bharatiya Janata Party leader and former prime minister A. B. Vajpayee suggested that the "general insecurity of menfolk" and their vested interests in "perpetuating male supremacy" lay at the heart of opposition to the bill.[24] Alva described what happened outside Parliament when the bill's opponents were worried that party leaders would pressure legislators to pass the bill. "Some senior M.P.s stood at the main gate of Parliament telling the arriving M.P.s, 'why have you come? Go away or your seat will go. You are mad.'"[25] In another revealing exchange, this time inside Parliament, an MP from an adjoining district tried to dissuade his colleague from endorsing the bill by threatening that he would eventually lose his seat. When Somnath Chatterjee (representing Bolpur) expressed support for the bill, Somnath Mohan Dev (representing Silchar) replied, "The Bolpur seat will become a woman's seat." Dev's appeal to fraternal solidarity failed, however, for Chatterjee answered, "If the Bolpur seat becomes a woman's seat and I am still in the reckoning, I will go to Silchar," implying that his support for the bill would give Chatterjee an electoral edge over Dev in Dev's own district.[26]

In the 2010 debates over the bill, anxiety over the loss of masculine political dominance manifested itself in several ways. Janata Dal (United) leader Mulayam Singh Yadav suggested, for example, that the Women's Reservation Bill might lead ultimately lead to an all-women parliament that would be "alarming" for the country.[27] Rashtriya Janata Dal leader Lalu Prasad argued that, given the impending passage of the bill, MPs should be given an increase in salary and pension because "many male MPs will lose their jobs once the women's reservation bill is passed."[28]

While the challenge to male dominance in the legislature alarmed some, others supported the bill for precisely that reason. As one reporter remarked, "The Lok Sabha, as every observant television viewer must have noticed by now, is an unabashed all-male club, or nearly so. In the forest of dhotis, kurtas, safari suits and shirts, the occasional sari or salwar kameez stands out for its rarity."[29] In one Lok Sabha debate, MP Krishna Bose echoed this comment, remarking that she felt "like an unwanted intruder in a male club."[30] Indeed, the focus on male domination of the legislatures led to large protests in support of the bill. In a mass rally in November 2001, for example, women demonstrators marched through the streets of the city of Patna shouting slogans like "vote hamara raj tumahara—nahi chalegi!" (our vote, your government—will not work!) and "Aawadi aadha aur shat pratishat—nahi chalegi!" ([men are] half the population, 100 percent of the voice—will not work!).[31] Such protests indicate that the fraternalist strategy of marginalizing women politically had backfired: Instead of diverting attention from masculinist rule, excluding women from the legislature had highlighted it.

"WHO WILL MAKE OUR DINNER?" UNSETTLING THE LINK BETWEEN WOMEN AND THE HOME

In addition to anxiety about the political sphere, the debates over the Women's Reservation Bill revealed worries that women's entrance into politics would threaten the link—both symbolic and real—between women and the home. According to one critic, women would be sullied by their engagement in the political sphere: "the actual experience with most states has confirmed the apprehension that reservation of seats for women has resulted in the womenfolk of the established leaders parading themselves as representatives of women with no improvement in performance and no reduction in corruption."[32] This argument reveals the instability of the identification of woman with the home; by entering politics, her own identification as woman would be called into question. Here, political involvement means the corruption of women themselves. Rather than women's entrance into political life being disruptive because of their symbolic embodiment of the private sphere, it is women's *failure* to represent the private sphere, these anxieties suggest, that the bill's opponents found so threatening.

To counter such objections, many of the bill's supporters offered romanticized imagery linking women to the home. They asserted, for example, that the presence of women in representational bodies would bring the "home" into public spaces and thus improve them.[33] The former Indian president K. R. Narayanan argued that "increased female representation would lead to heightened social sensitivity in legislative institutions. It would foster a greater sense of decorum and curtail the irksome tendency for aggressive and obstreperous behavior."[34] Women, in other words, would treat the nation as they cared for the family, with a focus on the well-being of its members. Nor was this argument restricted to male supporters of the bill. Pramila Dandavate held that because women "naturally think more about our families and our children," they would make "education, child welfare, and health" legislative priorities. "Unnecessary conflicts that are a drain on our resources will stop," she predicted.[35] Such arguments depicted women as potential redeemers of a violent and corrupt male political sphere. Women in Parliament would "instill meaning into what has degenerated into a purposeless institution," MP Maneka Gandhi claimed.[36] In this framing, women could bring their homemaking skills into political life. Women's role as mothers and homemakers would be maintained, in this configuration, but the number of their "children" would increase exponentially, their homes greatly expand.[37] Both of the positions within this strand of the debate thus equated women with the inner, private, domestic life of the nation, with the bill's proponents predicting that women's enhanced participation would have a redeeming and purifying effect on politics, and its opponents countering that women themselves (and thus the home) would be corrupted if women were to enter political life in large numbers.

There was another strand to the debates, however, one that focused explicitly on the inequitable power relations that restricted women to specific roles in the home. Opponents of the bill worried that it would challenge such power relations. One opponent, for example, argued that "once the bill passes, it'll be mother in the Lok Sabha and father in the kitchen."[38] MP Shivraj Patel, a supporter of the bill, decried this position, arguing that such arguments did "not do justice with their own family members."[39] Pramila Dandavate concurred. "I feel that our party wants women to be decorative pieces, like *achar* [chutney] with food or a flower pot," she said. "They do not want to share power in the real sense of the word. The male members joke about the issue but basically they feel threatened. . . . [They] ask in jest: Who will make our food?"[40] In this framing, the home is not an ideal sphere of harmony and nurture but a locus of gender conflict and domination. To opponents, the bill portended an unwanted challenge to male dominance in the home, an outcome that the bill's supporters welcomed. By highlighting the oppressive aspects of women's subordination in the home, this strand of the debate thus unsettled the equation of women and the home by exposing the hierarchies that sustained it.

PANDORA'S BOX OR EXPANDING CIRCLE?

While apprehensions about the Women's Reservation Bill were linked to questions of masculine dominance in politics and in the home, perhaps the most fraught issue has to do with the relationship between women's political empowerment and that of other marginalized groups in the Indian polity. Because of the internal hierarchies within the social group "women" and the close links between the postcolonial sexual and postcolonial racial contracts in the Indian context, questions of women's representation in the Indian parliament are inextricably linked to issues of caste and minority group representation.

Nivedita Menon notes that the issue of reserved seats for women cannot be thought of as a gender question alone, given its close relation to caste politics in India.[41] Since independence, low-caste groups have made extremely significant gains in political representation, due to a combination of constitutional provisions guaranteeing Scheduled Castes and Scheduled Tribes representation in Parliament, affirmative action measures, and, most important, the mobilization of these groups themselves. Although they have not addressed all the issues related to caste and tribal subordination, these advances have made India, in Zoya Hasan's words, "a success story with regard to the inclusion of excluded caste groups."[42] In addition to the SCs and STs, the "Other Backward Castes" (OBCs), castes that are not on the lowest rungs of the caste hierarchy but nonetheless have been socially, economically, and educationally marginalized, have also made impressive political gains. As a result of legislation passed in 1990 and 2006, OBC groups qualify for affirmative action measures such as allocations of government jobs and university admissions, but—unlike SCs and STs—not for reserved seats in the legislatures. Despite the absence of legislative reservations for OBCs, these backward caste groups have made sizeable electoral gains in recent years.

The debates over the Women's Reservation Bill are also closely linked to the question of the political underrepresentation of minority religious communities in India, particularly Muslims. In contrast to lower-caste groups that have made significant strides in representation, Muslims in India have been consistently underrepresented in national decision-making bodies. Although Muslims make up approximately 12 percent of the population, their representation in the Lok Sabha since independence has averaged only 5.79 percent. Muslim women have fared even worse; since independence only twelve Muslim women have been elected to Parliament. Zoya Hasan notes that such miniscule representation suggests that their participation has been hampered "both by their gender and their minority religious status."[43]

While Muslim underrepresentation can, in part, be attributed to such factors as the geographic dispersion of Muslim communities across India, the Constituent Assembly's removal of the measures that would have ensured their inclusion in national decision-making bodies has greatly restricted the discourse about how to remedy the situation. Hasan explains that attempts to implement affirmative action policies have been "blocked by the argument that minority development schemes militate against constitutional principles, which seek to make identities less salient for participation in the modern economy and politics."[44] Indeed, it is revealing that while several political parties supported the Women's Reservation Bill (in name if not in deed), there is no political consensus on establishing reservations for Muslims. The Indian government's Report on the Social, Economic, and Educational Status of the Muslim Community in India (commonly known as the Sachar Committee report, after Rajinder Sachar, the supreme court justice that Prime Minister Manmohan Singh appointed to oversee the committee), released in 2006, documented the extreme marginalization of Muslims in many areas of the polity but did not consider reservations as a remedy. According to Syed Shahabuddin, the Sachar Committee left "the heart of the problem untouched, the political empowerment of a persistently deprived community. . . . Without political empowerment no group in a multi-segmented polity can participate in governance or have a finger on the levers of the decision-making process or even enter the chambers where decisions are made."[45]

At the nexus of gender, caste, and minority group struggles for political inclusion, the debates over reservations for women in Parliament expose some of the fault lines between these movements and illustrate the continued salience of the politics of compensatory domination in postcolonial Indian politics. For example, the bill met with its most intense opposition from parties representing OBC groups, opposition that in large part blocked its passage for fourteen years. In one debate, Samajwadi Party chief Mulayam Singh Yadav, one of the most vocal opponents of the bill, cautioned that "amending the Constitution in the name of providing reservation to women is bound to open a Pandora's box as various sections of society . . . would also clamour for increasing the percentage of reservation in proportion to their population." Such a measure would, he warned, "destroy our political base."[46] Echoing Yadav's fears, Janata Dal chairperson Sharad Yadav warned, "do not open this Pandora's box."[47] Such reluctance to embrace women's expanded participation in politics suggests a failure to acknowledge the ways in which, in B. R. Ambedkar's words, "women are the gateways to the caste system," and that addressing women's subordination is central to undercutting caste hierarchies.

Likewise, instead of welcoming the measure and the opportunity it presented for challenging political marginalization on multiple lines of difference in addition to caste, male minority group leaders saw it as a threat. In one debate, for example, MP Shafiqur Rahman Barq suggested that the bill should not be passed because "the Muslim population will be at a loss and representation of Muslim population in the country will get a set back. . . . Injustice has been done to us so far in this country and if it is repeated then history and the House will not forgive anyone."[48] In the 2010 debates, MP Shri Abdul Wahab Peevee spoke persuasively about the need to give adequate representation to minority groups, but he opposed the Women's Reservation Bill, asking whether, "in future, we may have to have another Bill reserving 33 per cent seats for males if this trend continues in the House [for] if this trend continues, the male Members will be in minority here."[49]

The debates over the Women's Reservation Bill revealed, however, that the bill's proponents were not immune to the politics of compensatory domination themselves. Indeed, Nivedita Menon suggests that the Women's Reservation Bill was in part an attempt by upper-caste elites to shore up their power in response to gains by lower-caste groups, explaining that states that reserve seats for women have propped up the power of dominant castes. "When confronted with upper-caste concerns that seem to tie in with feminist concerns at the conjuncture," she writes, "the women's movement must make the moves necessary to undercut the upper-caste project."[50] In response to this dilemma, many women's groups have embraced the principle of "quotas within quotas," that is, the principle that within the number of seats allotted for women a portion would be set aside for women from lower castes and other marginalized groups. Reflecting an investment in majoritarian and upper-caste politics (despite the role of these politics in their own subordination as women and thus their own stakes in the politics of compensatory domination), however, some proponents of the bill have argued that the question of women's political marginalization should not be linked to issues of caste and minority group marginalization.

Some, for example, have asserted the singularity of women as a social group, urging legislators not to divide women by providing subquotas within the bill. Asked Margaret Alva, for instance, "There are currently no reserved constituencies for the Backward classes and minorities, so why should this issue get tied up with reservation for women?"[51] Subquotas for

Muslim women are an especially thorny topic of debate, even among those who advocated subquotas more generally. The BJP's Uma Bharti argued for subquotas for backward-caste women but not for Muslim women, because "in a secular Constitution, there can be no place for reservations based on religion" (Bharti did, however, advocate for subquotas for Muslim women from low or backward castes).[52] Others argued that questions of subquotas could be worked out in the implementation stage of the bill, after its passage. Kumari Mamata Banerjee, for example, explained that she and the bill's supporters were open to providing reservations for OBCs and minorities within the legislation, but asked her fellow members to "let the bill be introduced first."[53] Before her murder in 2001, Phoolan Devi protested her fellow women legislators' stand against subquotas. "It is regrettable," she said, "that my fellow sisters are not in favour of reservation on caste basis . . . to ensure [women's] proper participation in uplifting the society and it should be on the basis of their castes as scheduled castes, scheduled tribes, minority and backwards class, so that they may be relieved from further torture and exploitation."[54]

Laura Dudley Jenkins calls the phenomenon of groups working against one another's advancement in India the politics of "competing inequalities," in which competition over the allocation of benefits often divides groups that might otherwise work together to fight inequality.[55] This division among politically marginalized groups, Dudley explains, allows the dominant political parties to court the votes of women, lower castes, and minorities without making substantial concessions to any of these groups. These competing inequalities are more that simply the product of party machinations for electoral gain, however. They are both a product of the politics of compensatory domination and an instance of its contemporary practice. The postcolonial social contract has both dominatory and liberatory impulses. The politics of compensatory domination shores up the dominatory aspects of the postcolonial social contract and blocks efforts to foster the transformation of democracy on more inclusive grounds. But if groups have agreed to be ruled in part because this allows them the possibility of intra- or intergroup domination—in this case either masculinist, majoritarian, or upper-caste domination—then challenges to those modes of domination have the potential to transform the terms and conditions of political authority in India. Indeed, the uproarious scenes surrounding the passage of the Women's Reservation Bill point to the high stakes involved in the struggle to make good on the constitution's guarantees of political equality.

CALLING THE QUESTION: FROM RHETORIC TO GUARANTEES

The discussion of the Women's Reservation Bill prompted some of the most chaotic scenes in the history of the Indian parliament, causing adjournment on numerous occasions because of bedlam on the floor of the House. The highly emotional tone of the debates suggests the extent to which the bill threatened the foundations upon which political authority had rested in India. This specter of transformation produced deep anxiety. In his speech to Parliament against the bill, for example, MP Iliyas Azmi argued that it was a "ploy to destabilize the entire democratic system." Sharad Yadav warned his colleagues that "after fifty years of independence, the hornet's nest should not be disturbed by touching the issue [of reservations for women], otherwise the country's future will be bleak."[56] Mulayam Singh Yadav warned that the measure would "break the backbone of democracy" in India.[57]

As Yadav predicted, on several occasions the floor of the Lok Sabha resembled a hornet's nest or, in the words of one reporter, "a veritable battle field," with members rushing to the well, tearing up the bill before it could be introduced, scuffling among one another, and refusing to let one another speak.[58] A despairing I. K. Gujral, the former prime minister of India, commented after a particularly acrimonious day that "in the half century of our Republic, Parliament has never witnessed such indecorum. . . . I have had the opportunity of sitting in this House and the other House for the best part of my life. I have never witnessed such a scene." Reflecting upon another chaotic scene, in December 1998, the speaker of the Lok Sabha warned that "incidents of this sort strike at the root of the very credibility of this house and its survival and therefore are dangerous for our democratic polity."[59]

The uproar did not deter the bill's proponents. On the floor of the Lok Sabha in 2001, Margaret Alva declared that some might "believe that the aspirations of Indian women can be silenced by shouts and slogans against their rights, in the well of the House. But we are too many and too strong and too determined for that."[60] Alva's predictions proved true, and while the proceedings were no less tumultuous than the earlier debates, the Rajya Sabha approved the bill on March 9, 2010.[61] In doing so, the Rajya Sabha drew upon the liberatory impulse of the postcolonial social contract and began to make good on the constitution's guarantees of equality and inclusion in the political sphere. In the words of MP Shrimati Brinda Karat, in passing the bill the legislators had ensured that "the slogan of inclusion [would be] transformed from rhetoric to guarantees." Such a change, she added, would "not only address the long standing discrimination that women in India have faced in the political sphere, but also, I believe, deepen democratic processes."[62]

Matching the anxiety of the bill's detractors was the jubilation of its supporters upon its passage. One observer wrote that the passage of the bill had the effect of "rekindling in old timers the excitement of the day on which the newly passed Constitution of India was signed."[63] Several MPs paid tribute to male leaders like Ambedkar, Gandhi, Nehru, and Periyar, who saw the liberation of women as crucial to the nationalist project. They suggested that the bill represented a recommitment of Indian men to gender equality. Shrimati Brinda Karat, for example, paid tribute to the history of resistant convergence in India, noting that "as far as gender is concerned, it is a fact of history that in India it has not been male versus female . . . [and] some of the greatest social reformers in our country have been male." In the spirit of the renewal of the politics of resistant convergence, she acknowledged the crucial role of the "democratic-minded male" in getting the bill passed, saying, "I believe it is only fitting today that I congratulate all the men in this House, all the men in the country who have supported the bill."[64] Karat thus paid tribute to the resurgence of a politics of resistant convergence and suggested that its renewal was the key to the passage of the Women's Reservation Bill.

The struggle toward an inclusive, egalitarian politics in India is far from over, however. Indeed, the deepening of democracy involves contesting the contradictions of the postcolonial racial contract as well as those of the postcolonial sexual contract embedded in India's constitution. Such challenges will entail making good on the promise to address questions of caste and minority group political empowerment, as several supporters of the Women's Reservation Bill vowed to do once that bill was passed—for example, through measures such as the "quotas-within-quotas" approach. From the perspective of challenging the dominatory aspects of the postcolonial social contract, what is particularly appealing about such approaches to the Women's Reservation Bill is that they formally link women's empowerment to lower-caste and minority group empowerment, thus challenging the fragmentation of struggles for gender justice and caste and minority group rights. Further, such approaches call upon women to commit to low-caste and minority group political empowerment, and on low-caste and minority groups to commit to women's political empowerment, such that the principles of gender, low-caste, and minority group representation become mutually reinforcing.

5

Legal Pluralism and Gender Justice

In 1951, in a heated debate over Hindu law reform in newly independent India, B. R. Ambedkar, who had become the new government's first law minister, urged his fellow legislators to reform Hindu marriage law in a way that was congruent with the goals of liberty and equality. "If you mean to give liberty—and you cannot deny that liberty in view of the fact that you have placed it in your Constitution and praised the Constitution which guarantees liberty and equality to every citizen," he argued, "then you cannot allow this institution [of marriage] to stand as it is."[1] Ambedkar's arguments failed to persuade the majority of the House, and the reform was postponed. In protest, Ambedkar resigned his post, explaining:

> For a long time I have been thinking of resigning my seat from the Cabinet. The only thing that had held me back from giving effect to my intention was the hope that it would be possible to give effect to the Hindu Code Bill before the life of the present Parliament came to an end. I even agreed to break up the bill and restrict it to marriage and divorce in the fond hope that at least this much of our labour may bear fruit. But even that part of the bill has been killed, [so] I see no purpose in my continuing to be a member of your cabinet.[2]

Ambedkar's resignation from the cabinet reflected his despair, made more poignant by his own role in framing the constitution, over the inability of legislators to reconcile the discrepancy between women's legal subordination in Hindu personal law and the constitutional clauses guaranteeing their freedom and equality. Although he could not persuade the legislature to pass reforms, Ambedkar himself refused to participate in the fraternal alliance that supported such a contradictory resolution of the "woman question" in the postcolonial social contract.

Underlying the postcolonial social contract in India is a legal pluralist approach to governance in which separate religious groups or communities are governed by distinct laws in such family matters as marriage, divorce, and inheritance; for example, Hindu law (or "Hindu Code," as it is often called) governs Hindus in these matters, and Muslim law governs Muslims. This pluralist approach can be distinguished from a legal universalist approach in which a singular set of laws applies to all citizens of a polity.[3] In this chapter I argue that although the particular version of legal pluralism endorsed by the Indian constitution has discriminated against women, gender subordination is not a necessary feature of legal pluralism. I describe a competing, more liberatory version of legal pluralism that feminist and other progressive groups in India are working toward in order to reconcile group autonomy and gender rights as important collective goods.

HINDU LAW REFORM AND COMPETING APPROACHES
TO LEGAL PLURALISM

In contemporary political theory, the legal pluralist approach to jurisprudence is often seen not only in contrast to a legal universalist approach but in deep opposition to it. Further, legal universalism is frequently understood as fostering gender justice, while legal pluralism is often seen as enabling gender subordination. This association rests in part on the fact that legal pluralist regimes may (and often do) countenance group laws that discriminate against women, and on the fact that legal universalist claims are often made in the name of gender rights. An analysis of the struggles for gender justice in India, however, reveals two different forms of legal pluralism, what might be called "fraternalist pluralism" and "egalitarian pluralism." While gender and other forms of intragroup subordination constitute fraternalist pluralist modes of jurisprudence, egalitarian pluralism challenges such subordination.

Fraternalist and egalitarian legal pluralism both share an embrace of the law as an important arena for group differentiation and autonomy in a multicultural framework. What marks a particularly "fraternalist" form of legal pluralism are substate (group, community, or territorial) laws that discriminate against women (or other vulnerable subgroups). These laws legitimate masculinist authority in the name of group preservation and differentiation. Similarly, fraternalist legal pluralism engenders masculinist allegiance to the state to the extent that the approach countenances or fosters gender domination. In contrast, an egalitarian legal pluralist approach emphasizes intragroup equality and justice. While sharing with fraternalist legal pluralism a commitment to group-differentiated law, egalitarian pluralism works against the politics of compensatory domination because it actively rejects intragroup rule. From an egalitarian pluralist perspective, the state's legitimacy lies in the extent to which it supports equality and justice both within and among groups. It is this form of pluralism that animated, in part, the reform of personal law in the resistant convergence of feminism and nationalism in the struggle against British rule in India. From an egalitarian legal pluralist perspective, British rule was illegitimate not only because of its "foreignness" but also because of the ways that the British supported, solidified, and exacerbated hierarchies within and between groups.

These two contending forms of legal pluralism can be seen in the debates over Hindu law reform in postindependence India. The Hindu Code Bill, formulated by the Rau Committee and published in 1946, is an example of egalitarian pluralist legislation. The bill was drafted with the intention of "bringing the most progressive elements in the various schools" of jurisprudence that governed Hindu family life.[4] As opposed to an earlier version of Hindu Code reform in which very few women were consulted, roughly 25 percent of the witnesses the Rau Committee interviewed were women. Geraldine Forbes writes that the committee's final report recommended a set of reforms that combined the most progressive elements and interpretations of the ancient Hindu texts with contemporary legal principles. Tanika Sarkar notes that "the changes suggested in the code were nothing more than an attempt to improve the rights of Hindu women and give effect to the fundamental right that there should be no discrimination based on sex." The Hindu Code Bill, as originally formulated, sought to ground Hindu personal law in the most egalitarian of the diverse strands of Hindu thought and practice, what Flavia Agnes calls the "best of all laws" approach to codification.[5]

As discussed in chapter 3, the Constituent Assembly postponed consideration of the Rau Committee's Hindu Code Bill until after independence, given the intense opposition to it. In 1951 progressive congressional leaders attempted to get the marriage and divorce sections of the bill through the provisional legislature. They decided to omit the sections that concerned women's right to inheritance, anticipating, as Arundhati Roy Choudhury explains, that "the succession clause, which impinged directly on the dominant male preserve, would be opposed strongly, whereas monogamy and the right of divorce would meet with less opposition."[6] The arguments for the bill in this round of debate were explicit about the goal of gender justice. Ambedkar, for example, argued against the gender inequality in the Hindu practice of sacramental marriage. "I am quite convinced in my own mind that no man who examines that institution in a fair, honest, and liberal spirit can come to the conclusion that it satisfies either the ideal of liberty or of equality," he said. "I want to put one question to the House. Are we for slavery or are we for free labour?"[7]

As in the Constituent Assembly, filibustering and fierce debate in 1951 stalled and ultimately killed even the marriage and divorce sections of the bill. As Ambedkar put it, Hindu law reform "was killed and buried, unwept" in the provisional parliament.[8] Reforming Hindu personal law remained an issue after the first Lok Sabha was elected in 1952, but the shape of the debate changed dramatically, shifting from a focus on women's equality to one on community consolidation. "After the 1952 elections," Choudhury writes, "the government seemingly gave up all its talk on gender justice. . . . Now the Hindu law bill was projected as a means to unify the nation. The government explained that the reform of the Hindu law was being brought forward with an ideology aimed at bringing together all Hindus."[9] J. Duncan Derrett notes that this approach grew out of the Congress Party's theory that "all Hindus form one community," a theory, Derrett explains, that was questionable in the sphere of religion "but in the field of law was patently false."[10] Indeed, Madhu Kishwar describes the push for Hindu Code reform after 1952 as "part of the process of consolidating Hindus as Hindus."[11]

The Hindu law reforms that were eventually passed, although they alleviated gender inequality in some ways, represented a deeply compromised form of egalitarian pluralism. In addition to the shifting rhetoric regarding the reform of Hindu personal law, the later reform proposals departed in several respects from the principle of legal equality for women. The reforms, passed in 1955–56, consisted of several acts: the Hindu Marriage Act, the Changes in Guardianship Act, the New Maintenance Act, and the Hindu Succession Act. After their passage, as Madhu Kishwar points out, these acts were touted "as the symbol of the new government's supposed commitment to the principles of gender equality and non-discrimination enshrined in the Constitution." But in fact they represented an ambiguous victory for women's rights in India, for they failed to establish gender equality and left women significantly disadvantaged vis-à-vis men—for example, with respect to rights of succession. In some instances, Kishwar explains, women actually lost rights that they had enjoyed under customary

law, because the legislators "road-rolled out of existence a number of func-
tioning local and regional legal systems, several of which provided better
rights to women in several respects."[12] For example, the Hindu Succession
Act specifically excluded agricultural landholdings from its scope, though
this exclusion eroded the customary rights that some women—women
from lower castes, in particular—had had to agricultural land.[13]

The consolidation of the Hindu community through Hindu law reform
reveals the limits of the pluralism envisioned in the constitution. Susanne
and Lloyd Rudolph note that "the reformation of personal law itself led
toward uniformity within each of the compartments. To assert that there
is one undifferentiated 'Hindu' and 'Muslim' personal law was itself a
significant act of homogenization. The personal law of Hindu lower and
upper castes differs markedly, as does law between regions which have different kinship systems."[14] Although the legislation was pluralist from the
perspective of the state, from within the different religious communities
the reforms tended toward uniformity rather than heterogeneity. Unfortu-
nately, in moving toward uniformity, the reforms did not incorporate the
"best of all laws" of the different practices in existence at the time of the
reforms.[15] Indeed, Agnes notes that "through an active collusion between
patriarchal premises of the state and the manipulation of male relatives,
women of the lower community were disempowered of their rights over
property."[16] A more robust, more egalitarian legal pluralist approach would
not only have countenanced these more gender-just customary practices
but would have incorporated them into the code itself.

That the reforms in Hindus personal law were passed at all, however,
even in their compromised form, indicates a shift in the terms and conditions of the postcolonial social contract for Hindus. The reforms illustrate
the possibility of a legal pluralism that resolves the contradiction between
the fundamental right of gender equality promised by the constitution and
the reality of legal subordination on the basis of gender. That the discourse
of community consolidation could allow reforms in the direction of gender
justice shows the potential of the group itself to become the basis for egalitarian solidarity.

On a more ominous note, however, the shift in the framing of Hindu
personal law reform from gender justice to community consolidation facilitated a Hindu majoritarian politics within which women themselves are
deeply implicated.[17] As I discuss below, the Hindu Code reform became a
rhetorical weapon against Muslims in the hands of fundamentalist Hindu
parties that used it to argue for a uniform civil code based on the reformed
Hindu Code.

THE SHAH BANO CASE AND SHIFTING APPROACHES
TO FRATERNALIST PLURALISM

Although the legislature initiated reforms in Hindu law, it did not do the same for Muslim, Christian, or Parsi personal law in early postindependence India, instead pursuing a policy of noninterference in these communities' personal law. After the trauma of Partition, Zoya Hasan explains, the government was particularly reluctant to involve itself in matters of Muslim personal law and risk alienating the Muslim leadership; "the government conceded the ground to the Muslim leadership on this vital issue in the hope that this would ensure their loyalty and support."[18] Similarly, the government made no attempt to reform Christian or Parsi personal law during the wave of Hindu law reform in the 1950s. Until 1970, the marriage law that applies to Christian Indians (who constitute roughly 2 percent of the population) was linked to English marriage law, such that any changes in English law would be automatically incorporated into Indian Christian law. The Parsis, a very small but economically very powerful minority, reformed their personal laws in the 1930s but did not do so again until the 1990s.

Although women's groups had been fighting discrimination against women under postindependence personal law for many years, the Shah Bano case propelled the issue to the forefront of public controversy in the 1980s. Shah Bano, a Muslim woman, sued for maintenance from her husband when he divorced her after forty-three years of marriage. Her ex-husband argued that since he had paid her maintenance for three months and given her the *mehr* (an amount agreed on before marriage), he had fulfilled his obligation to her under Muslim personal law. The case reached the Supreme Court, which in 1985 ruled in Shah Bano's favor and awarded her a monthly maintenance amount 179 rupees, a sum that the court thought was necessary to prevent her from becoming destitute. Madhu Kishwar explains that this was not the first Supreme Court ruling to award maintenance to divorced Muslim women and cites the Bai Tahira case of 1979 and the Fuzlumbi case of 1980 as precedents. In both of these cases, however, Muslim personal law was not the focus of the judgment; in fact, Kishwar notes, in the Bai Tahira judgment, the court did not "even mention the word 'Muslim' but instead emphasized that if the amount of *mehr* paid to the divorced woman is insufficient to prevent her from becoming destitute, the court will stipulate the amount that is needed."[19] Although the justices ruled in favor of the divorced woman in both these cases, the rulings themselves provoked very little protest. In the Shah Bano decision, however, the court, in its ruling, interpreted the Koran, made disparaging comments about Muslim personal law, and called for enactment of a uniform civil code. Many observers saw the decision as a direct attack on legal pluralism itself.

In response to the ruling, Muslim religious leaders led huge protest marches around the country. In response to the protests, Rajiv Gandhi's government passed legislation designed to mollify the Muslim leaders. Called the Muslim Women (Protection of Rights on Divorce) Bill, the bill undid the impact of the Supreme Court ruling by absolving the Muslim husband of the responsibility to pay maintenance to his divorced wife.[20] In passing this bill, the government acquiesced in Muslim religious leaders' demands and ignored liberal and progressive opinion within the Muslim community. As Zoya Hasan observes, the government thus reinforced the "assumption that Muslims are a religious community, that the theologians are its sole spokesmen, and that there exists a clear equation between law and community identity." The government in this instance affirmed a fraternalist approach to legal pluralism, an outcome particularly damaging to women; as Hasan notes, "from the standpoint of women the difficulty lies in the constant emphasis on the unity of community identity, defined in terms of family codes. . . . Whatever rights they might have achieved are thus sacrificed at the altar of 'Muslim identity.'"[21]

The Shah Bano case and the subsequent government intervention through the Muslim Women (Protection of Rights on Divorce) Bill marked a significant shift in the ruling Congress Party's approach to governance. Instead of the noninterference that had characterized early postindependence approaches to minority personal law reform, the government's involvement in the Shah Bano case marks what Ashutosh Varshney calls a turning point from a policy of "equidistance" to a policy of "equiproximity" to India's religious communities.[22] In order to avoid antagonizing either the Hindu or the Muslim community, the government attempted to woo them both by catering to their communal sentiments; concessions to one community required "equal" concessions to the other. Hasan describes the deal struck between Rajiv Gandhi and Maulana Ali Nadavi, a leading Muslim theologian, as exemplary of this political bargaining. "Rajiv Gandhi agreed to concede his demand to revoke the Shah Bano verdict on [Nadavi's] express assurance that he and the Muslim Personal Law Board would not involve themselves in the Babri Masjid dispute. Muslims would obtain a revocation of the court verdict through Parliament and Hindus would be granted darshan [a sacred viewing] at the Ram Janmaabhumi by unlocking the gates of the Masjid." Together, "these two decisions . . . were part of a 'grand' Congress strategy of using religious issues and sentiments to regain its hold over Hindu and Muslim votes."[23] In this exchange the government catered to the most communal elements of both communities in the name of secularism and helped set the stage for the devastating communal riots at Ayodhya in 1992–93. That the Muslim religious leaders agreed to the compromise—unlocking the gates of the Masjid in exchange for the protection of personal law—reflects the continued compensatory power of the subordination of women in stabilizing relations of rule at the center, and the steep price that the "bargain" at the heart of the postcolonial social contract continues to exact from both women and minority groups.

Just as the government's response to the Shah Bano dispute strengthened the most conservative elements of the Muslim community, it also consolidated the power of nationalist groups within the Hindu community. Not only was the site of the disputed mosque/temple at Ayodhya opened to them as a result of the controversy, but they also manipulated the terms of the debate to foster the image of "a conservative, inward-looking and backward Muslim community."[24] Furthermore, the Hindu Right, led by the Bharatiya Janata Party, used the controversy to portray Muslim women in particular as in need of their protection. Zakia Pathak and Rajeswari Sunder Rajan describe the agenda here: "the protection of women of a minority community [Muslims] thus emerges as the ploy of a majority community to repress the religious freedom of that minority and ensure its own dominance."[25] Such paternalist discourse, coupled with communal violence, made it harder, however, for women and others to struggle for gender justice. After fighting her case for ten years, for example, Shah Bano asked for the withdrawal of the Supreme Court ruling in her favor because she "did not want to be the cause of anti-Muslim riots." Madhu Kishwar explains that, "even while strongly acknowledging the injustice done to her as a woman, she felt compelled to give up her struggle in order to save her community from attack by Hindu fundamentalists."[26]

In the wake of the Shah Bano controversy, the Hindu Right took up the issue of a uniform civil code as an important part of their political agenda. When the BJP contested and won the national elections as a leading member of the National Democratic Alliance coalition in 1998, the introduction of a uniform civil code became one of the BJP's three "contentious issues" (the other two being the construction of a Ram temple on the disputed site in Ayodhya and the abrogation of article 370 of the constitution, relating to Kashmir). In asserting their commitment to a uniform civil code, their leader argued that "separate personal laws only perpetuate gender inequality."[27] Kishwar, however, argues that Hindu nationalists only feigned interest in women's rights, masking their true interest in formulating a uniform civil code based on Hindu ethics.[28]

Flavia Agnes explains further that "while the portrayal of a barbaric Hindu provided the justification for the colonial interventions in the pre-independence period, the image of the backward, pre-modern, and polyga-mous Muslim served the Hindu communal forces in the post-independence period." Agnes suggests that at the root of Hindu ire about Muslim per-sonal law is not so much gender justice as fear that polygamy might lead to the faster growth of the Muslim population.[29]

MOVING TOWARD EGALITARIAN PLURALISM

While the Shah Bano case and its aftermath strengthened conservative groups within both the Hindu and the Muslim communities, it also invigo-rated the struggle for egalitarian legal pluralism. Indeed, in contemporary Indian politics, feminist and other progressive groups are promoting sev-eral different strategies toward gender-just personal laws on the personal, group, and state levels. These struggles have included taking advantage of loopholes in personal laws to encourage egalitarian relationships; promot-ing personal law reform within Hindu, Muslim, Christian, and Parsi com-munities and pressuring the state to pursue egalitarian interpretations of law; and developing an optional egalitarian civil code.

In the wake of the Shah Bano controversy, progressive and other wom-en's groups have pursued the strategy of working with the personal laws as they are in order to build egalitarian relationships. This approach takes advantage of room for maneuvering within existing personal laws, in which the terms are not necessarily dictated by the state or community. This approach stresses the potential, even within the highly constrained contexts of state and community-backed discrimination, to use opportuni-ties within social life as it stands for individuals to determine the terms and conditions of their relations with one another. With respect to Muslim personal law, for example, progressive groups advocate using the tradi-tional marriage agreement at wedding ceremonies to assert that the wom-an's right to divorce would be equal to the man's, without going against Muslim personal law. Munira Merchant, in a report entitled "Divorce Among Indian Muslims," notes that there is always a marriage agreement, or *nikahnama*, at Muslim wedding ceremonies. Since the Koran prescribes no uniform form of *nikahnama*, the parties involved can specify, for exam-ple, "that the man cannot practice polygamy, that the woman's right to divorce would be equal to that of the man, and that *mehr* would be paid immediately after divorce"—all of these things without breaking the letter of Muslim personal law. Such a strategy, of course, is never "free"; Merchant points out that this strategy depends on grassroots education and awareness if women and men are to exercise this option in an egalitarian vein.[30] Feminist groups have worked to establish gender-just marriage agreements as a community norm by pressuring the All India Muslim Personal Law Board (AIMPLB) to put forth a model *nikahnama*. In 2005 the AIMPLB finally agreed, and although the model *nikahnama* it recommended fell short of feminist demands (only discouraging triple *talaq* rather than making it equally available to women or forbidding the practice, for example), it nonetheless gave important community backing to some principles of gender justice. The continuing political challenge for social movements is to create more such opportunities for self-determination within personal laws and elsewhere and to encourage egalitarian relations within them.

On the state level, women have lobbied the state to interpret even discriminatory personal laws in their favor. For example, Muslim women have used the Muslim Women Act in numerous cases to extend their rights to maintenance after divorce. "Right from 1988," Flavia Agnes explains, "the courts have engineered women's rights through innovative interpretation of the new statute, ushering in a new set of rights within the established principles of Muslim law." Agnes argues that both the mainstream and alternative media have tended to ignore these efforts, in part because they challenge the notion of the Muslim woman as victim. Agnes urges us to read efforts by Muslim women to seek redress through the courts as acts of assertion. "Divorced Muslim women had to fight every inch of the way for their rights," she points out, "right from the trial courts in small district towns up to the supreme court. And they withstood the ordeal with courage and determination."[31] Indeed, in part as a result of these struggles, Werner Menski writes, the Muslim Women Act has "morphed by now into an aggressive system of post-divorce provisions for Indian ex-wives."[32]

While these strategies focus on fostering gender-just change within personal laws as they stand, another approach has been to redouble efforts to reform personal laws themselves from within the different religious communities. This strategy affirms the possibility of building gender-just communities in a pluralist framework. Its logic hinges on the notion that the institutionalization of group-based jurisdiction over matters relating to family relations—that is, the existence of the system of personal law itself—leaves space for substate democratic collectivities in which egalitarian relations could be fostered. The area of Hindu law that feminists and other groups have primarily focused on has been extending women's rights to inheritance, especially with respect to joint family property. In 2005 the Indian parliament, under pressure from these groups, passed an amendment to the Hindu Succession Act that enabled daughters to inherit joint family property. As Menski explains, under this legislation "Hindu daughters shall be entitled to equal inheritance as their brothers in the Hindu joint family from birth."[33] This legislation represents a momentous change in Hindu personal law, although much work remains to be done to make this shift a reality in practice as well as in law.

With respect to Muslim personal law, areas that Muslim women have worked especially hard to reform include modifying the practice of unilateral, extrajudicial divorce (the triple *talaq*), banning or regulating the practice of polygamy, and extending women's rights to inheritance, divorce, and maintenance. For Christian women, pressing issues have included establishing the right to divorce for Christian women on similar grounds with Christian men (while Christian men can divorce their wives on charges of adultery, Christian women have to prove two offenses—adultery and cruelty—on the part of the husband) and extending women's rights to inheritance and maintenance. Parsi women's reform efforts have focused primarily on issues related to inheritance and maintenance.

An important part of the work of reforming personal laws involves challenging the notion of an assumed consensus within the respective communities about the laws themselves. Highlighting dissent within each community has meant publicizing support for reform and building more such support. Sabeeha Bano, for example, conducted a survey among a sample of Muslim women in New Delhi and found that more than 80 percent of respondents believed that the systems of triple *talaq* and polygamy should be reformed. The group Muslim Intelligentsia also held a convention for the purpose of building "a consensus in the community on the issue of triple divorce." In addition to condemning the practice of triple *talaq*, which "allows a casual attitude towards women" and violates "Koranic instructions," the members of the convention also set up a committee charged with pressuring the Muslim Personal Law Board to convene a conference of Islamic jurists, Muslim intellectuals, and opinion makers to "evolve an authentic interpretation on the issue, keeping in mind the ground social realities."[34] Amrita Chhachhi notes that one drawback of attempting reform from within is that activists can get "stuck in a maze of interpretations of the shariat [religious doctrine]," and that it depends on the willingness of the *ulema* (religious leaders) to agree to demands for change. Chhachhi cites the example of feminists in Pakistan, who felt that "this strategy backfired since it sanctioned the authority of religion in determining women's status in society." Instead, Chhachhi recommends building alliances with other women's groups in South Asia. "The dilemmas over personal law and minority interests," she writes, "could be overcome if women's groups in Pakistan, Bangladesh and India jointly put forward a Charter for Women's Rights." Such a joint project, she argues, could help "overcome the present chauvinist, xenophobic basis of national and communal identities" by constructing a broader South Asian identity.[35]

Muslims feminists have also set up parallel legal institutions as a strategy in developing a consensus to counter conservative interpretations of the law. When faced with the continued intransigence of the AIMPLB on issues of gender justice, for example, a group of Muslim women formed their own Muslim Personal Law Board in 2005.[36] Its general secretary, Parveen Abdi, argued that such a board was necessary because "women have gone through hell. They became victims of incest, they faced forced marriages, whimsical talaqs and biased judgments. There seemed to be no one to take up the suffering woman's cause, not least the AIMPLB."[37]

The importance of building social consensus for legal reform of the different personal laws is highlighted by Mary Roy's experience in 1986 in opposing the Travancore Christian Succession Act, which held that a "daughter shall receive a quarter of the share of a son or Rs. 5000/-, whichever is less." The Supreme Court ruled in Roy's favor and struck down the act. In an article written six months later, Roy lamented that "only two women, copetitioners in the case that I filed, have filed petition suits." The main barrier to women in her community seeking redress through the courts," she wrote, lay in "the sad fact . . . that most women will quietly sign away their rights. They have been well trained. Those who do have doubts will need just a little twist of the arm to be coerced into signing on the dotted line." The harassment that Roy was subjected to by her own family exemplifies the social reprobation faced by women who choose to go against this training; Roy described her family's reaction to the judgment as ranging from "utter and total embarrassment" to open hostility. "This is the price I have to pay for defying social customs," she wrote, adding, "the family is backed by the bishops and the community."[38] She was not "run out of town," she said, only because she was a respected headmistress of a local school, but others, she points out, lack that kind of advantage. "If women have not the money and staying power to fight a long drawn out legal battle through several courts, facing animosity at every step, where will they find sustenance?"[39]

EGALITARIAN PLURALISM AND NONPATERNALIST UNIVERSALISM

The final egalitarian pluralist strategy to be considered here is the attempt to fashion an optional egalitarian civil code at the national level. Although early feminist struggles against women's legal subordination focused on developing a uniform civil code that would establish one set of laws for all Indians, many Indian feminist groups are now wary of this approach to gender equality. This wariness stems in part from the fact that the Hindu Right has made the enactment of a uniform civil code part of its platform (in what many see as an effort to subordinate differences between communities to a Hindu-dominant conception of morality), as well as from skepticism about the desirability or efficacy of state-centered modes of working toward gender justice. Instead of a uniform civil code that would abolish the system of personal law altogether, many feminist and progressive groups are pushing for the establishment of an optional egalitarian civil code that could be used when people feel that their personal laws are discriminating against them. Nivedita Menon explains that personal laws would usually prevail in this approach, but that in "times of dispute women would have the choice of opting for the [egalitarian civil] code." A related proposal, put forth by the Working Group on Women's Rights in Delhi, uses the strategy of "reverse optionality," in which all citizens would be covered by an egalitarian, gender-just common law but could choose instead to be governed by personal laws, if they wished, and would always have the option of returning to the framework of common law.[40] Both of these strategies hinge on giving people the choice of pursuing relief from discrimination through either state or community mechanisms.

This concept of an optional and egalitarian civil code pushes contemporary theories of pluralized governance in productive directions. One influential articulation of this approach is Ayelet Shachar's model of "joint governance," which gives people choice with respect to jurisdictional authority. Joint governance, Shachar explains, recognizes that "some persons will belong to more than one political community" and rejects the "misguided premise that a single entity [either the state or the community] be granted *exclusive* jurisdiction over the individual." Shachar calls the premise of exclusive jurisdiction "absolutist" and outmoded. In her view, identity groups—groups, such as religious or cultural groups, that "share a comprehensive world view that extends to creating a law for the community"—can provide the grounds for a polity that pluralizes sovereignty.[41] Shachar argues for what she calls a "transformative accommodation" variant of the model of shared governance that would provide for overlapping jurisdiction between identity groups and the state in such predetermined matters as education, family law, and so on. In Shachar's model, individuals have the option of pursuing remedies through either the state or the identity group; such choice would exert pressure on both the group and the state, because both would be competing for people's allegiance.

For Shachar, the problem of intragroup hierarchy is partially solved, because an individual who is ill served or dominated by her or his identity group can turn to the state for relief. Likewise, if the individual suffers discrimination from the government, she or he can seek redress within the jurisdiction of the community group. Shachar believes that the joint governance model would put pressure on both the state and identity groups to become more egalitarian.

> Since the two (group and state) now engage in a competitive relationship (where the result of failure to address their constituents' needs can lead to the strengthening of the other power holder), both authorities are put under that much more pressure to serve and retain their constituents *within* their respective spheres or submatters. . . . The empowerment potential of joint governance lies in its ability to make visible the enduring structures of in-group power relations. . . . Once historically vulnerable group members have been given the means to withstand the oppressive tendencies of their traditions and the opportunity to self-select their jurisdictions, group leaders may finally start recognizing the need to avoid internecine conflict. This in turn can stimulate *nomoi* [identity] communities to earn their allegiance, rather than merely inheriting them, because the stakes of the group survival have become so much higher.[42]

In Shachar's framework, there would be an open door between the state and the community that would enable people to escape oppressive relations. Although Shachar has confidence that the state and identity group would compete for the loyalty of vulnerable individuals, however, the reverse is also possible: State and identity group leaders could cooperate to reinforce each other's control over individuals. The potential for this kind of situation is increased by the fact that state and identity group hierarchies often overlap and that those who hold power in one arena often hold power in the other as well. Indeed, as the history of both colonial and postcolonial politics in India (and elsewhere) demonstrates, one state-building strategy has been to court the allegiance of elite group members by reinforcing their in-group dominance through the politics of compensatory domination. The challenge of a joint governance approach lies in finding ways to guard against such reinforcing hierarchies and the politics of compensatory domination.

The feminist approach to addressing the legal subordination of women in India—namely, by enacting an optional egalitarian civil code—fits well with Shachar's joint governance proposal in that both approaches advocate individual choice in a situation of plural jurisdictions. Rather than assume a well-meaning state, or one vulnerable to pressure from the structural competition of joint governance, however, Indian feminists seek to create an explicitly gender-just framework from the outset. This approach circumvents the problem of reinforcing hierarchies by ensuring the existence of at least one collective entity grounded in egalitarian relations.

This approach also has the advantage of offering an optional rather than a mandatory civil code, which should open avenues to challenge inequitable relations of rule within families and communities that are not dependent on the mandatory extension of the state's own authority into those realms. This aspect of the approach is particularly important, given the location of the issue of the uniform civil code at the intersection of postcolonial racial and sexual contracts. One of the central worries about the uniform civil code is that discourses of gender equality rights are a cover for the extension of the authority of a Hindu-dominant state into a sphere of minority group autonomy. In part, this is a fear of what could be called "paternalist universalism," in which the discourse of protection—in this case, protection of women—is used to extend the reach of state authority. Rather than the politics of compensatory domination that marks fraternalist modes of legal pluralism, paternalist universalism is marked by the politics of protective domination. The principle of choice provides a check on the politics of protective domination. In a sense, the very element of choice in the proposed egalitarian code calls the state's bluff: Does the state's stake in issues of gender justice lie in the extension of its own authority or in the extension of democratic relations themselves?

Werner Menski argues that postindependence developments in personal law have led not to the unification of different groups under a singular civil code but to the "harmonization" of different personal laws with the principles of gender rights laid down in the constitution. Such harmonization points to the potential congruence between an egalitarian legal pluralism and a nonpaternalist universalism. Universalism and legal pluralism both have a dominatory and a liberatory mode; the liberatory modes of each can interlock in the service of autonomy and equality.

One of the strengths of the triple-pronged Indian feminist approach to egalitarian relations on the interpersonal, group, and state levels is that while each component reinforces the others, it does not necessarily depend on the existence of the others. For example, in the absence of an egalitarian civil code on the state level, an egalitarian personal law approach can enable people to circumvent state-backed or state-tolerated subordination. If both the state and the group constrain the creation of egalitarian relations, the approach directs attention to opportunities on the personal or individual level that can potentially help people shape their relations in egalitarian ways. These multiple approaches can thus be seen as complementary, each working to broaden the choices available to women in an egalitarian pluralist framework. Taken together, the proposals emphasize change from within communities and within relationships, with recourse to the state as an option. The different approaches work toward an egalitarian legal pluralist framework in which cultural autonomy and gender equity are coexistent. Fraternalist pluralism hinges on the compensatory subordination of women in such a way that gender justice becomes antithetical to cultural, group, and religious autonomy. Feminist activists' refusal of this fragmentation destabilizes the logic of fraternalism as a mode of domination and points to the possibility of an egalitarian pluralism in which gender equity and religious and cultural autonomy are linked goals.

Conclusion: Building a Nondomination Contract

In their efforts toward legal equality and an inclusive political sphere, feminist and other progressive activists have both drawn upon and advanced the Indian framers' promise to build "the fullest" democracy in India and have worked to resolve the postcolonial social contract's contradictions in a liberatory direction. In addition to challenging gender, caste, and minority group subordination in the Indian polity, their approaches to social justice point to new configurations of the social contract more generally. Indeed, if the paradigmatic agreement in social contract theory is an agreement to be ruled, struggles to deepen Indian democracy can be seen as generating agreements *not* to rule on the interpersonal, group, and state levels. Taken together, such agreements can form the basis of what might be called a "nondomination contract," an expressly egalitarian reformulation of the social contract that fosters the participatory construction of social and political solidarity.

The notion that there could be an emancipatory reconfiguration of the social contract is contested in critical contract theory, and a central question for critical contract theorists is whether the notion of social contract should be kept as a normative device or be discarded altogether. Charles Mills argues for keeping it, on the grounds that the idea of a social contract can be a mechanism for egalitarian transformation, despite its use as a tool of subjection and marginalization. Mills suggests that the fundamental principles of social contract theory—its premise that state and society are human creations and that we are all fundamentally free and equal—can be mobilized to argue for justice and inclusion. In contrast to the ways in which women, the poor, and people of color have been excluded from the social contract, he argues that we can build a truly inclusive contract. This new contract, he suggests, *"will require a fundamental rethinking of the depiction of the creation of society and what real egalitarianism now morally requires of us."*[1]

Whereas Mills advocates for a more inclusive social contract, Carole Pateman warns that using the language of contract to work for social and political transformation is extremely risky. In Pateman's view, the contract is the particularly modern mechanism by which relations of domination and subordination take on the guise of freedom, on both the individual and the collective levels. In a discussion with Mills about this point in their co-authored *Contract and Domination,* she explains that "the point of the social contract is that in the modern state individuals give up their right of self-government to another or a few others."[2] What legitimates this move is that these individuals have supposedly agreed (explicitly or implicitly) to be so ruled. Indeed, in her earlier work *The Problem of Political Obligation,* Pateman notes that the paradigmatic agreement in social contract theory is quite particular (and peculiar): it is a promise to obey. Instead of contract, she suggests that we explore new models of free agreement as a mode of constituting our social and political relationships. "Why introduce contract at all?" she asks. "Why not start by trying to move to another model of free agreement? . . . Why not find other terms for 'free agreement talk' that also convey the meaning of a voluntary mutual undertaking and offer some hope of moving away from all the associations and assumptions of 'contract'?"[3] For Pateman, the concept of the social contract cannot escape its baggage as a mechanism of domination and subordination. In the words of Audre Lorde, the social contract is an example of a "master's tool" that cannot be used to rebuild the "master's house."[4] Instead of a new social contract, Pateman urges us to build our political and social houses with the brick and mortar of free agreement.

These two approaches are not necessarily incompatible. The struggles for egalitarian pluralism in India can be seen, in part, as fostering arenas in which people are free to agree on the terms and conditions of their own relationships, a move consistent with Pateman's emphasis on the importance of free agreement between people as a liberatory mode of constituting social and political relationships. The push for an optional egalitarian civil code, an important part of the struggle against the legal domination of women, can be seen as an effort to generate a collective commitment to legal equality at the state level, a move in tune with Mills's call for an egalitarian reformulation of the social contract. Taken together, these approaches can be thought of as constituting a "nondomination contract," an egalitarian formulation of the social contract that creates space for the participatory construction of social and political solidarities based on agreement.

Whereas Mills and Pateman debate the extent to which the social contract should be claimed for liberatory ends, Wendy Brown suggests that the notion of social contract has lost its purchase in contemporary political life altogether. Rather than rely on a fiction of consent, she argues, the contemporary liberal state legitimates its authority in the absence of "viable alternatives." "Legitimation is procured, at least provisionally, through the absence of viable alternatives. . . . Not the autonomy of the originally willing subject—to which even most contemporary liberal theorists do not subscribe—but the patent unhappiness of the former Soviet or Somali subject is tendered as proof (enough) of the supremacy of liberal regimes." In Brown's view, contract theorists, even critical ones, are focusing on an outmoded form of political legitimation; such legitimation, she argues, is "now achieved through the 'self-evident' superiority of rights discourse and constitutional government to all other modalities of political order and disorder."[5] Brown's point that the liberal state is assumed to be a self-evident good in much of contemporary political discourse (or at least that it is the best that we can do) is apt enough, but it is precisely under such conditions that critical social contract theory has value. In such a context of seemingly few choices, critical contract theory can be a useful tool for interrogating the limits of current political arrangements, as well as for articulating alternatives. One of the harmful effects of Eurocentrism in political theory is that compelling alternatives, whether achieved or actively sought, are often downplayed or dismissed as appropriate only in certain contexts. Using critical contract theory to highlight postcolonial challenges to exclusionary and dominatory political orders works against this myopia, and indeed against the colonial history of contract itself. Brown notes that contract language operated historically "to legitimate, even inspire, colonial and imperial domination by articulating the superiority of Euro-Atlantic political cultures over those subjugated by them."[6] If the notion of a social contract has been used to legitimate colonial rule, it can now be used to focus attention on egalitarian approaches to political solidarity and to help generate a sense that other forms of democracy are indeed possible.

TOWARD AGREEMENTS NOT TO RULE

In this section, I translate struggles to deepen democracy in India into the language of contract in order to make these strategies more legible as alternate modes of configuring political solidarity and authority. This move involves interpreting political intervention in a way that focuses on the terms and conditions of political solidarity and authority. If political solidarity and authority are imagined as grounded in an agreement, what kind of agreement does the intervention foster or invite? I examine each of the egalitarian pluralist interventions on the interpersonal, group, and state levels and suggest ways in which these efforts to end gendered legal domination might be interpreted as fostering agreements not to rule.

On the interpersonal level, the egalitarian pluralist approach focuses attention on people's opportunities to shape and construct personal rela- tions on terms of their own making. Contemporary approaches to com- bating women's legal subordination in India highlight the possibility for relational self-determination and egalitarian agreement even within con- texts of state and community-backed discrimination. The work that Muslim feminists are doing in developing the egalitarian exercise of *nikahnama* (the practice in Muslim personal law in which marriage partners agree on the terms and conditions of their relationship) is a particularly good example of this approach. Progressive groups are encouraging partners to ground their relationships in egalitarian commitments—for example, to pledge that the woman's right to divorce will be equal to the man's. This kind of promise can be seen as an agreement not to rule in that the parties specifically cede the right of domination, even when that right is legally available. Because the state gives the right of determining marriage law to the community, and because the community itself recognizes the *nikahnama*, such pledges would be legally enforceable. This is not to say that such an agreement is easy or unconstrained; certainly state and community norms still obtain, and the parties have to do the difficult work of defying family, community, and collective pressures in order to make such an agreement.

The egalitarian pluralist approach also fosters agreements not to rule at the group level. On this level Indian feminists are working to reform personal laws within different religious groups. One reason why reli- gious groups in India offer such promise for challenging the politics of compensatory domination and cultivating egalitarian relations is that the major religious groups already enjoy significant autonomy from the state in the area of personal law. Indeed, just as there is space within certain personal laws for people to establish partnerships grounded in egalitarian relationality, the institutionalization of group-based jurisdiction over family relations—that is, the existence of the system of personal law itself—cre- ates the possibility for members of those groups to participate in setting the terms and conditions of their association. Although current personal laws in India tend to discriminate against women, understanding how the equation of group autonomy and control over women has enabled group subordination—that is, understanding how compensatory domination has undermined both minority group and women's rights—could propel the movement toward intragroup democracy.

Finally, the efforts of Indian feminists to enact an optional egalitarian civil code can be seen as a move to generate an agreement not to rule on the state level. In practice, this commitment to egalitarianism entails two implicit agreements. The first involves one's own relationships: One agrees not to rule over someone else if that person does not agree to be ruled. The second involves a commitment on the collective level to ensure that others have the option of freeing themselves from relations of domination if they so desire. In the Indian context, the optional egalitarian civil code would do this work legally by providing a means of jurisdictional exit if a member of a religious community felt subordinated by his or her community's personal laws.

It is important to note that the extensive space for the exercise of autonomous relationality on the interpersonal and substate levels embedded in the egalitarian pluralist framework leaves open the possibility of domination; paradoxically, one could agree to be ruled. An optional egalitarian civil code would ensure that a key condition of autonomous relationality in this framework is that the individual or group member has the option to free him- or herself from discrimination or subordination, and the one exercising the domination be required to relinquish this power. In this formulation of the social contract, one cannot be (as in the Rousseauian social contract) "forced to be free," but one can be forced *to free*. The role of both the state and social movements would be to ensure that exit options were legally, psychically, economically, socially, physically, and politically viable.

Taken together, all three levels of intervention can be understood as fostering a model of political authority and solidarity geared toward egalitarianism—in other words, a nondomination contract. Comparing the nondomination contract to both the fraternalist and paternalist approaches to the social contract reveals important differences between them. Whereas at the base of both the fraternalist or paternalist social contracts is a singular agreement to be ruled, the nondomination contract is constituted by multilevel agreements not to rule. In a fraternalist approach to the social contract, for example, submission to political authority is engendered by a politics of compensatory domination in which political actors consolidate or exacerbate inter- and intragroup hierarchies and elite group members agree to be ruled in order to rule over others at the substate level. In a paternalist approach to the social contract, an agreement to be ruled is mobilized through a politics of protective domination in which vulnerable groups agree to be ruled in order to avoid being ruled by others at the sub-state level. I have argued in this book that although seemingly opposed, these two approaches are closely linked, and that political authorities rely on a complex interplay of both approaches in order to mobilize consent. In contrast, in a nondomination contract, people agree not to rule one another on the interpersonal and group levels and the state backs up these agreements by offering legal and material resources that enable people to avoid or exit relations of domination.

What might motivate a person to make agreements not to rule? How can a person learn to want to avoid domination, especially if such domination appears to be in her or his own economic, political, or psychic interest? One motivation, surely, is a commitment to the well-being and flourishing of others. The motivation does not have to be solely other-oriented, however. Another, perhaps equally compelling motivation is a recognition of the costs of the politics of compensatory domination and the ways in which intra- or intergroup authority at the substate level comes at the price of submission to inequitable relations of rule at the state level. Analyzing the ways in which the state supports, secures, or consolidates relations of domination within and between groups in order to secure its own authority can make intra- and intergroup hierarchies less enticing by both denaturalizing the hierarchies themselves and highlighting the price of compensatory domination to those who are enticed into such rule. Reflection on the ways in which powerful members of subordinate groups allow themselves to be dominated in exchange for the opportunity to dominate others leads to sticky questions of complicity, but it may also motivate resistance in that it inspires us to ask the question: Whose commands do people have to follow in order to exercise command themselves?

The nondomination contract is grounded in the recognition that a commitment to one another's freedom is a commitment to our own, and that one can agree not to rule in part so as not to be ruled oneself. This formulation of the social contract directs our attention to the ways in which our relationships are implicated in interlocking sets of hierarchies but can also be sources of resistance that resonate across these lines of power. As such, challenging the politics of compensatory domination and working toward more egalitarian relationships and collectivities necessitates the critical interrogation of our own and one another's particular insertion into these hierarchies. An example of such work is that of the Sangtin Collective, a group of women in India who work together to analyze their own lives in terms of gender, caste, class, and communalism. These women observed that "whenever we reflect deeply and collectively on a set of personal or structural issues, that reflection ceases to be a critique of a specific individual or organization. It becomes connected to all those social, economic, and political conditions and processes within which we are living."[7]

On the state level, what might motivate political authorities to move in the direction of a nondomination contract? Here, the lessons of colonial and postcolonial Indian politics are instructive: It is possible to maneuver the interplay between the fraternalist politics of compensatory domination and the paternalist politics of protective domination to push the state toward more egalitarian outcomes. Doing so, as both colonial and postcolonial history exemplifies, requires refusing the temptation of consolidated or augmented inter- or intragroup power and privilege offered by the fraternalist approach. By refusing these fraternalist alliances, movements call the question on the paternalist approach, pressuring state actors to make good on the rhetoric of empowerment embedded in the discourse of protective domination. For example, in the struggle to extend the franchise to women, discussed in chapter 2, Indian men refused the masculinist alliances fostered by the colonial state and voted overwhelmingly to allow women to vote. Colonial state actors had to honor that outcome; if they had refused, their paternalist promises to protect women would have been exposed as patently false—mere rhetoric.

CROSSING CONTEXTS

While this book has focused mainly on the Indian political context, I turn now to the United States in order to demonstrate how the notion of a nondomination contract can be applied across political contexts. For the U.S. context, a multilevel nondomination contract offers ways to link together a variety of political interventions on the interpersonal, group, and state level.[8] Further, conceptualizing these varied interventions as linked efforts toward a nondomination contract highlights their importance for the egalitarian reconfiguration not only of particular relationships and collectivities but also of political authority itself. On the interpersonal level, the notion of the nondomination contract focuses attention on the possibilities in people's relational lives (in homes, workplaces, schools, communities, and other contexts) that might enable them to generate egalitarian relations with one another. Egalitarian norms for relationships in these contexts may already exist or they may need to be constructed. Thinking about the U.S. political context, for example, feminists and other social reformers have worked to create more possibilities for egalitarian relations within intimate partnerships. This work has meant transforming the marriage contract as well as making the choice to live together outside marriage more acceptable and achievable. According to the 2000 census, approximately 11 million people in the United States live with an unmarried partner, a tenfold increase from 1960 (in Europe, where health and other benefits have been decoupled from marriage and employment, cohabitation rates are even higher).[9] In addition, strategies to reform the marriage contract have included amending or challenging laws that foster inequality within marriage as well as shifting cultural expectations about marriage such that relations of command and obedience are seen as symptoms of abuse, a breach of the marriage contract, rather than a right that contract establishes.[10] From writing their own vows, to the equitable distribution of cooking, cleaning, and child-care responsibilities, to terminating partnerships under "no-fault" divorce clauses, people are doing the everyday work of setting the terms and conditions of their own intimate relations. The trend toward greater freedom in determining those terms and conditions is embattled in the United States, of course; people confront laws in several U.S. states (albeit rarely enforced) that prohibit people from cohabiting, defense-of-marriage legislation that would prohibit most gays and lesbians from getting married at all, and the linkage of health care, citizenship, and welfare benefits to marriage in ways that often compel intimate partners to marry. In general, though, transforming the marriage contract, as well as making "living together" economically, culturally, and politically possible, has been one area in which reform efforts have met with success in creating more autonomous and egalitarian modes of relationality. Other equally pertinent examples of egalitarian intervention on this level include attempts to create nonauthoritarian homes and classrooms for the upbringing and education of young people, and efforts to foster nonhierarchical modes of decision making in workplaces.

On the group level, a multitiered nondomination contract highlights the potential of substate collectivities (identity groups, religious groups, schools, labor unions, political groups, neighborhoods) to challenge hierarchical intra- and intergroup norms. In the United States and elsewhere, identity groups resisting oppression on the basis of race and gender have been important substate collectivities that have oriented group members toward the possibility of social change. Feminists of color and theorists of intersectionality have called attention to the ways in which the most powerful subgroups within an otherwise subordinate group, such as white women in the category women, or men of color within the group people of color, both participate in and gain power and privilege from a racist patri-archal order, even while that order subordinates and marginalizes them.[11]

One example of a challenge to those intra- and intergroup power relations in the United States is the work that feminists of color and others have done to address violence against women of color. Organizations such as Incite! Women of Color Against Violence have criticized ways in which the main-stream movement against violence against women in the United States cen-ters on white women's concerns and relies on a law enforcement approach to addressing questions of interpersonal violence. Such an approach, these organizations argue, does not take up ways in which communities of color are targeted and brutalized by the police in the United States. These orga-nizations have also criticized the ways in which the movement against state violence against people of color focuses on the needs and concerns of men of color and largely ignores questions of violence against women. To address these critiques about both movements, organizations like the harm-free-zone collectives in New York City and Durham, North Carolina, have devel-oped community-based approaches to addressing violence against women that do not rely on the police or the state.[12] Like the reform of personal laws within religious communities, this approach affirms the possibility of build-ing autonomous, gender-just communities from within.

Finally, a nondomination contract emphasizes the importance of a commitment to egalitarian relations at the collective or state level. Such an approach directs collective attention to addressing the legal, material, and psychic conditions that keep people in nonegalitarian relationships or collectivities. Although struggles for the collective provision of economic security, health care, education, and child care are often (and correctly) seen in terms of struggles for justice, rights, and care, there is also a case to be made for them in terms of democracy, insofar as these issues often compel people to stay in relations of domination and subordination in the home, workplace, neighborhood, or other community settings.

A CRITICAL CONTRACT APPROACH TO DEMOCRACY AS NONDOMINATION

The notion of nondomination has been pivotal to several contemporary the-ories of democracy and government. Phillip Pettit, for example, argues that freedom is best understood as nondomination and that democracy plays a key role in promoting and defending such freedom. Ian Shapiro goes even further, asserting that a commitment to nondomination is fundamental to the definition of democracy; "democrats," he suggests, "are those who share an interest in avoiding domination."[13] For oppressed or marginalized groups, linking democracy and nondomination has tremendous appeal; it makes their subordination in any arena antithetical to democracy itself.

Thinking of a polity as potentially grounded in a multilevel nondomination contract can amplify and extend this notion of democracy as nondomination in several ways. One of the critiques of contemporary theories of nondomination holds that although its proponents are committed to eradicating domination in all areas of life, they generally focus on the state as the locus of change and transformation.[14] One strength of the multilevel approach embedded in the nondomination contract I have described is that it is not dependent on the state for its enactment. Although generating a state commitment to nondomination through legal reform and other measures is a central goal, the state is not the only (or even the primary) locus of democratic transformation. The nondomination contract can be practiced in the here and now, in our everyday lives, with or without the support of the state (and sometimes in opposition to it). Indeed, as discussed earlier, egalitarian interventions on the substate level, such as the reform of personal laws from within or community-centered antiviolence efforts, have great potential to foster democracy as nondomination.

Another way that a critical contract approach contributes to the theorization of nondomination is by moving away from the literature's disabling dependence on a notion of "common interests" or "basic interests." Pettit, for example, writes that "the promotion of freedom as non-domination requires . . . that public decision-making tracks the interests and the ideas of those citizens whom it affects."[15] David Watkins points out that this emphasis on shared interests among citizens means that Pettit's theory is relatively hampered in providing insight about what to do in situations where there is no identifiable common interest—in deeply divided societies, for example.[16]

In Shapiro's framing, what marks a demand for obedience as legitimate is whether the demand is linked to the notion of the other's "basic interests," and whether domination occurs when an authority exercises a right of command against these basic interests. He explains that "compliance is often compelled in armies, firms, sports teams, families, school, and countless other institutions. . . . [But] there is a world of difference between a teacher's requiring a student to do her homework and his taking advantage of his power position to engage in sexual harassment of her. The latter is domination, but the former is not. Hierarchical relations are often legitimate, and, when they are, they do not involve domination on my account."[17]

By linking legitimacy to a notion of "basic interests" and institutional purview, Shapiro opens a loophole for paternalism in his theory, a space where one may act according to his or her own appraisals of another's basic interests, the other's own conception of those interests notwithstanding. Shapiro's definition of domination is worrisome in that it leaves open a space for such skepticism about people's ability to identify and act upon their basic interests in a manner they themselves define. Indeed, the notion of legitimate hierarchy tied to a notion of basic interests assumes that one may not always be able to articulate one's basic interests, that basic interests themselves are "basic" enough so as to be recognizable across lines of difference, that one's basic interests are more or less congruent with one another (so that one usually would not have to choose—or be forced to choose—between them), and that one must always act according to one's basic interest. It is because the student might not fully comprehend the ways in which doing her homework is in her basic interest, for example, that the teacher may legitimately command her to do so. It might be argued that the paternalism of Shapiro's example makes sense because he is referring to an adult-child relationship—a legitimately paternal relationship—and that children do indeed need guidance to understand and act upon their basic interests (though this assumption itself is open to contestation); however, the other legitimate relations of hierarchical command and control that Shapiro points to in business firms, armies, and sports teams involve relations between adults. Further adding to the troublesome nature of Shapiro's paternalist loophole is that although Shapiro himself does not delineate those who are in the position to command and those who should obey according to class, race, and gender, the institutions in which he suggests that domination can legitimately be exercised certainly (if often implicitly) do so. The notion of the nondomination contract closes the paternalist loophole in Shapiro's approach by asserting that domination obtains when a person or group can determine the actions of another either directly or indirectly in such a way that goes against the other's agreement.

Contemporary theorists of democracy as nondomination have themselves been critical of social contract approaches to political legitimacy. Pettit, for example, is wary of contract as a mechanism of establishing social, economic, and political relations because of the potential for people to enter into domination contracts for reasons of economic necessity or ideological or social pressure.[18] In a critical contract approach to democracy as nondomination, hierarchies based on agreements to be ruled would also be highly suspect. But rather than invalidate agreement as a sound basis for relationships, the questions that skepticism about such agreements prompt would focus on the terms and conditions of agreement to relations of domination and on the presence or absence of viable exit options.

Shapiro is wary of the notion of social contract as well. In his view the social contract approach rests on an improbable fiction of a preorganized polity and both depends on and perpetuates an unrealistic and undesirable emphasis on consensus.[19] In contrast to a disabling emphasis on consensus, generating and sustaining agreements not to rule depends on viable modes of expressing and acting on dissent by enabling significant autonomy in the creation of the terms and conditions of interpersonal relations. Furthermore, far from a fiction of prepolitical organization, people forging a nondomination contract must refigure existing political communities or generate new ones. In this account, engendering a nondomination contract involves real people agreeing not to rule among themselves and backing up those agreements on the collective level.

UTOPIANISM AND THE IMPORTANCE OF IMAGINED ALTERNATIVES

The alternative social contract described here is still very much the object of contestation and struggle. That a nondomination contract is still an imagined alternative instead of an achieved one makes it no less worthy of consideration; indeed, utopian alternatives are vital for political transformation. In *At the Heart of Freedom*, Drucilla Cornell distinguishes between two modes of utopian thinking. The first is grounded in perfectionism that seeks to impose a "blueprint for a good society," even if it is "out of touch with what is possible for actual human beings to live out in their daily home, work, or public lives." Cornell firmly rejects this mode of utopianism but embraces another, which functions to "represent the separation of right from reality, and to maintain the critical edge that delimits the conflation of the two." This latter form, what might be called "critical utopianism," is based on the notion that "what is possible cannot be known in advance of social transformation." "Utopianism has always been tied to the imagination, to visions of what is truly new," Cornell explains. "Yet what is possible always changes as we change with the transformations we try to realize. Is it mere fantasy, or is the presence of the dream *itself* not proof enough that it might be possible? At last it is up to us to turn yesterday's utopia into a new sense of reality."[20]

A critical social contract approach to democracy as nondomination rests on a critical utopian confidence in the possibility that people can develop and sustain egalitarian relations with one another. Such a possibility is, of course, constrained both externally and internally, but a particularly democratic hope lies in thinking that these constraints—institutionally supported hierarchies, for example, or senses of self-worth and modes of subjectivity that hinge on relations of command and obedience (or coerced consent)—are neither inevitable nor desirable.[21] Critical utopian terrains are terrains of risk and vulnerability; in addition to envisioning and constructing frameworks that foster autonomous and egalitarian relations, we can develop our confidence in one another and in ourselves as having the potential for such relations by sharing stories of democratic possibility with one another. This book has focused on movements in colonial and postcolonial India that have worked or are working against the politics of compensatory domination in ways that point in the direction of more egalitarian forms of political solidarity. What possibilities for egalitarian engagement do we see in our political struggles, in our neighborhoods, in our workplaces, in our families, in our classrooms, in our imaginations, in our senses of self?

In his political manifesto *Hind Swaraj,* Mahatma Gandhi analyzed British colonial rule in India and argued that "the English have not taken India, we have given it to them. They are not in India because of their strength, but because we keep them."[22] Gandhi's insight suggests the extent to which consent is not only a normative concept but also a descriptive one: Political authority depends upon our consent, or at least our acquiescence. Indeed, some of the most successful struggles of the last century—the movement for Indian independence from British colonial rule, for example, or the civil disobedience campaigns of the U.S. civil rights movement—point to the tremendous power that groups can exert to challenge inequitable relations of rule by withholding consent and refusing to acquiesce in them. While these victories offer hope, the reassertion of control over women as a central term of exchange after Indian independence suggests the need for caution: We must pay close attention to the terms and conditions of "consent" and seek new bases for democratic solidarity that do not depend on racial, religious, caste, class, or gender subordination. The story of the postcolonial social contract reminds us that we must insist on democracy's possibilities, while challenging the compromises enacted in its name.

NOTES

INTRODUCTION

1. India, Constituent Assembly, *Debates*, 1:62.

2. Mills, *Racial Contract*, 6.

3. Ibid., 13–14.

4. Although the forms that social contract stories can take are very flexible, all such stories serve in some way to either legitimate or interrogate terms of political authority or solidarity.

5. Flax, *American Dream in Black and White*, 4.

6. Pateman and Mills, *Contract and Domination*, 215.

7. Mills, "Race and the Social Contract Tradition," 3.

8. Foucault, "Nietzsche, Genealogy, History," 163.

9. Pateman and Mills, *Contract and Domination*, 4.

10. Fraser, "Beyond the Master/Subject Model," 180.

11. Pateman and Mills, *Contract and Domination*, 15.

12. Rousseau, "Discourse on the Origin of Inequality," 77.

13. While Rousseau focuses on state authority, contemporary feminist theorist Deniz Kandiyoti's work on interfamilial "patriarchal bargains" offers a similar insight about the micropolitics of household life. In her observations of Indian familial structures in "Bargaining with Patriarchy," Kandiyoti acknowledges the tremendous ideological, social, economic, and political pressures on women to submit to relations of subordination in the family, but she also suggests that women acquiesce, in part, so as to sustain domination over those beneath them in family hierarchies.

14. Scott, *Domination and the Arts of Resistance*, 82.

15. Rousseau, "Discourse on the Origin of Inequality," 77.

16. Caste in India is a hereditary system of stratification based on endogamy (intergroup marriage). One's caste, or *jati*, is associated with one's occupation, and upper castes tend to hold profound material, social, and political power over lower castes. Although associated primarily with Hinduism, some Muslims and Christians also adhere to the caste system. For an excellent discussion of the relationship between caste and gender in India, see Chakravarti, *Gendering Caste Through a Feminist Lens*.

17. According to the 2001 census, approximately 80 percent of Indians are Hindu, 13 percent Muslim, 2 percent Christian, and almost 2 percent Sikh. There are also a significant number of adherents of Buddhism, Jainism, Animism, Zoroastrianism, and Judaism. Although the right to freedom of religion is enshrined in the constitution, which calls for the equal treatment and tolerance of all religions, "communalism" (that is, conflicts between religious groups) has often marked postcolonial politics.

18. Members of tribal groups—called *adivasis*—constitute approximately 8.2 percent of the population. These groups are recognized in the constitution as eligible for affirmative action measures.

19. Mills, *Racial Contract*, 27.

20. Bhargava, *Secularism and Its Critics*, 3.

21. Spivak, "Can the Subaltern Speak?" 297.

22. Chatterjee, *Nation and Its Fragments*, 120.

23. Chatterjee himself downplays the women's movement in India, which is surprising given his otherwise extremely insightful analysis. I argue that one of the reasons why he does not give it more attention is that his exclusive focus on colonial paternalism prevents him from seeing the importance of challenges to colonial fraternalism as well.

24. Winant, *World Is a Ghetto*, 1, 31, 134, 9.

25. Baber, "'Race,' Religion, and Riots," 701, 713. See also the Sachar Committee Report (India, Committee on the Status of Women in India, *Towards Equality*) for a detailed description of the social, economic, and educational marginalization of the Muslim community in India, in part resulting in what the committee notes is the increasing "ghetto-ization" of the community.

26. Alexander and Mohanty, *Feminist Genealogies, Colonial Legacies*, xxx.

27. Ibid., xxxvii.

28. Spivak, "Criticism, Feminism, and the Institution," 9.

29. Lugones, "Heterosexualism and the Colonial/Modern Gender System," 186.

30. See, for example, Lugones, *Pilgrimages/Peregrinajes;* Kelley, *Race Rebels;* and Scott, *Domination and the Arts of Resistance.*

31. Brown, "What Has Happened Here?" 298.

CHAPTER 1

1. Mehta, *Liberalism and Empire*, 200. While Mehta focuses on the collusion of liberal thought and empire, see Muthu, *Enlightenment Against Empire*, and Pitts, *Turn to Empire*, for excellent studies of anti-imperialist strains within liberal thought.

2. Spivak, "Can the Subaltern Speak?" 297.

3. Stoler, "Carnal Knowledge and Imperial Power," 52.

4. Pateman, *Sexual Contract*, 78.

5. Stein, *History of India*, 224. British attempts to court Indian elites often met with resistance. For example, Brahmins initially refused to teach British scholars Sanskrit. Tony Ballantyne observes that "in this context, silence was a potent reminder of indigenous agency and the limits of British power." Ballantyne, *Orientalism and Race*, 23.

6. Dirks, *Castes of Mind*, 9.

7. Rocher, "British Orientalism in the Eighteenth Century," 222.

8. Stein, *History of India*, 222.

9. Muller quoted in Trautmann, *Aryans and British India*, 176.

10. Ibid., 17. See also Ballantyne, *Orientalism and Race*, 41–44.

11. Baber, "'Race,' Religion, and Riots," 707.

12. Ballantyne, *Orientalism and Race*, 50.

13. Patankar and Omvedt, "Dalit Liberation Movement," 413.

14. Jones to Arthur Lee, October 1, 1786, in Jones, *Letters of Sir William Jones*, 712–13.

15. Jones to GJS, the Second Earl Spencer, February 20, 1791, ibid., 885.

16. Jones quoted in Cannon, *Life and Mind of Jones*, 349.

17. Hastings quoted in Trautmann, *Aryans and British India*, 17.

18. Galanter, *Law and Society in Modern India*, 23.

19. Hastings, "Plan for the Administration of Justice."

20. Trautmann, *Aryans and British India*, 63.

21. Kishwar, "Codified Hindu Law," 2146.

22. Dirks, *Castes of Mind*, 34.

23. Agnes, *Law and Gender Inequality*, 24.

24. Derrett, *Religion, Law, and the State in India*, 233.

25. Agnes, *Law and Gender Inequality*, 23–24.

26. Ibid., 44.

27. Chakravarti, "Whatever Happened to the Vedic Dasi?" 30.

28. Calman, *Toward Empowerment*, 149.

29. Mani, *Contentious Traditions*, 32–34, 29, 38.

30. Kumar, *History of Doing*, 9.

31. Mani, *Contentious Traditions*, 21.

32. Nandy, *At the Edge of Psychology*, 4.

33. Lugones, "Heterosexualism and the Colonial/Modern Gender System." See also Oyewumi, *Invention of Women*.

34. Lugones, "Heterosexualism and the Colonial/Modern Gender System." See also Allen, *Sacred Hoop*.

35. Agnes, *Law and Gender Inequality*, 41–57.

36. Sharpe, *Allegories of Empire*, 29.

37. Dirks, *Castes of Mind*, 33.

38. Grant, "Observations on the State of Society," 60.

39. Grant quoted in Trautmann, *Aryans and British India*, 103–4.

40. Grant, "Observations on the State of Society," 25, 2.

41. Pandey, *Construction of Communalism*, 49.

42. Grant quoted in Dirks, *Castes of Mind*, 33.

43. Mill quoted in ibid., 36.

44. Ibid.

45. Mill, *History of British India*, 280.

46. Majeed quoted in Dirks, *Castes of Mind*, 32.

47. Stein, *History of India*, 221.

48. Other important Anglicist policy measures that heralded a shift from a fraternalist to a paternalist approach included the introduction of English-language education and new policies of racial endogamy.

49. Kumar, *History of Doing*, 9.

50. Bentinck quoted in Mani, *Contentious Traditions*, 24.

51. Stein, *History of India*, 224.

52. Quoted in ibid., 219.

53. Bentinck quoted in Mani, *Contentious Traditions*, 29.

54. Ibid., 15.

55. Mill quoted in Trautmann, *Aryans and British India*, 120, 119.

56. Spivak, "Can the Subaltern Speak?" 297.

57. Kumar, *History of Doing*, 10.

58. Chakravarti, "Whatever Happened to the Vedic Dasi?" 34.

59. Mani, *Contentious Traditions*, 40.

60. Agnes, *Law and Gender Inequality*, 47.

61. Sinha, *Colonial Masculinity*, 4.

62. Mani, *Contentious Traditions*, 5.

63. Mills, *Racial Contract*, 27.

64. Mani, *Contentious Traditions*, 41.

65. Shohat and Stam, *Unthinking Eurocentrism*, 15.

66. See Parel and Keith's groundbreaking collection of essays, *Comparative Political Philosophy*; and Mehta, *Liberalism and Empire*, 216.

67. Shohat and Stam, *Unthinking Eurocentrism*, 16.

68. Dallmayr, "Beyond Monologue," 249.

69. See Thomas, "Orientalism and Comparative Political Theory," for a discussion of the linkages between present-day comparative political theory and Orientalist modes of knowledge production.

70. Shohat and Stam, *Unthinking Eurocentrism*, 16.

71. Ari Fleischer, White House press secretary, press briefing, November 27, 2001, http://www.presidency.ucsb.edu/ws/index.php?pid=47606.

CHAPTER 2

1. For an excellent discussion of how some Western women worked with nationalists and feminists to fight colonialism and women's subordination in South Asia, see Jayawardena, *White Woman's Other Burden*.

2. Sarkar, *Modern India*, 4.

3. Chatterjee, *Nation and Its Fragments*, 120.

4. Sangari and Vaid, "Recasting Women: An Introduction," 12.

5. Jayawardena, *Feminism and Nationalism in the Third World*, 7.

6. Mani, *Contentious Traditions*, 5.

7. Sarkar, *Hindu Wife, Hindu Nation*, 36.

8. Both men quoted in ibid., 46.

9. Forbes, *Women in Modern India*, 31, 70, 72.

10. Kazi, *Muslim Women in India*, 11.

11. Menon, *Gender and Politics in India*, 8.

12. Cousins, *Indian Womanhood Today*, 27.

13. Gandhi quoted in Kishwar, "Gandhi on Women," 1692.

14. Kazi, *Muslim Women in India*, 11.

15. Ambedkar quoted in Patankar and Omvedt, "Dalit Liberation Movement," 413.

16. Irschick, *Politics and Social Conflict in South India*, iii.

17. Barnett, *Politics of Cultural Nationalism in South India*, 321.

18. Hardgrave, *Essays in the Political Sociology of South India*, 25.

19. Ramasami, "Genesis of My Self-Respect Movement," 11.

20. Pandian, *Caste, Nationalism, and Ethnicity*, 63.

21. Ambedkar quoted in Patankar and Omvedt, "Dalit Liberation Movement," 413.

22. Lakshmi, "Mother, Mother Community," 75.

23. Quoted in Devendra, *Status and Position of Women in India*, 137–38.

24. Ibid.

25. Montagu, *Indian Diary*, 115–16.

26. Chattopadhyaya, *Awakening of Indian Women*, 49.

27. Chaudhurani quoted in Forbes, *Women in Modern India*, 94.

28. See Mahan, *Women in Indian National Congress*, 214.

29. Ibid.

30. India, Franchise Committee, *Indian Constitutional Reforms*, 4–5.

31. Reddi and Cousins quoted in Mahan, *Women in Indian National Congress*, 220 and 216, respectively.

32. Cousins, *Indian Womanhood Today*, 219.

33. Reddi, *Speeches and Writings*, 2:4.

34. Cousins, "What Women Have Gained by the Reform," 97. Indeed, women were admitted to the British electorate in 1918, after sixty years of struggle, but suffrage was restricted to women over the age of thirty. The franchise was not granted to all women until 1928.

35. Chatterjee, *Nation and Its Fragments*, 131, 133.

36. Sinha, *Specters of Mother India*, 159.

37. Quoted in ibid.

38. Chattopadhyaya, "Oral History," 71.

39. Nehru quoted in Mahan, *Women in Indian National Congress*, 303.

40. *Indian Annual Register*, 274.

41. Ibid., 278.

42. Sarkar, *Modern India*, 4, xxii.

43. Forbes, *Women in Modern India*, 115.

44. Sinha, *Specters of Mother India*, 220.

45. Ibid.

46. Basu and Ray, *Women's Struggle*, 46.

47. Ibid., 48.

48. Ali quoted in Forbes, *Women in Modern India*, 114, 116.

49. Basu and Ray, *Women's Struggle*, 67.

50. Forbes, *Women in Modern India*, 116, 118–19.

51. Ali, *Emergence of Feminism*, 152–53.

52. Forbes, *Women in Modern India*, 120.

53. Ultimately, the India Act of 1935 increased the ratio of women-to-men voters from 1:20 to 1:5 by implementing a variety of administrative measures, such as including in the electorate wives of men who were eligible to vote.

54. Sinha, *Specters of Mother India*, 199.

55. Ibid., 244.

56. Ibid., 244, 243.

57. Crenshaw gives several examples of how antiracist and feminist movements in the United States have marginalized the concerns of women of color by focusing on the concerns of white women in the category "women" and men of color within the group "people of color." Crenshaw, "Mapping the Margins," 357–58.

58. LaClau and Mouffe, *Hegemony and Socialist Strategy*, 183–84.

CHAPTER 3

1. Nehru's speech can be found in India, Constituent Assembly, *Debates*, 1:62.

2. Sarkar, *Modern India*, 1.

3. Stein, *History of India*, 315–36.

4. Constituent Assembly, *Debates*, 1:6.

5. Mills, *Racial Contract*, 12, 3.

6. Rau, *India's Constitution in the Making*, xliii.

7. Winant, *World Is a Ghetto*, 134.

8. Mills, *Racial Contract*, 127.

9. Constituent Assembly, *Debates*, 1:281, 89.

10. Bajpai, "Constituent Assembly Debates," 1843.

11. Constituent Assembly, *Debates*, 1:298.

12. Ibid., 1:47, 338.

13. Kaushik, "Women and Political Participation," 43.

14. Basu and Ray, *Women's Struggle*, 28.

15. Constituent Assembly, *Debates*, 1:140.

16. Ray, "Oral History," 31.

17. Constituent Assembly, *Debates*, 1:138.

18. Ibid., 2:278 (Pandit), 8:350 (Patel).

19. Bhargava, "Democratic Vision of a New Republic," 52–54.

20. Hasan, *Politics of Inclusion*, 3.

21. Constituent Assembly, *Debates*, 1:57.

22. Ibid., 2:302 (Pataskar), 7:306 (Rasul).

23. Gandhi, *Hind Swaraj and Other Writings*, 188, 28, 189.

24. Constituent Assembly, *Debates*, 5:58.

25. Ibid., 4:548.

26. Brass, "Strong State and the Fear of Disorder," 60, 66.

27. Bajpai, "Constituent Assembly Debates," 1837.

28. Constituent Assembly, *Debates*, 7:911.

29. Bajpai, "Constituent Assembly Debates," 1840.

30. Constituent Assembly, *Debates*, 5:270.

31. Ibid., 4:641.

32. Ibid., 11:797.

33. Austin, *Indian Constitution*, 80.

34. Constituent Assembly, *Debates*, 7:357.

35. Guha, *India After Gandhi*, 235–36.

36. Constituent Assembly, *Debates* [legislative], 2:866.

37. Constituent Assembly, *Debates*, 7:541.

38. Ibid., 7:544.

39. Ibid., 11:656.

40. Misra, *Making of the Indian Republic*, 22.

41. Pateman, *Sexual Contract*, 78, 102.

42. Ibid., 2.

43. Committee on the Status of Women in India, *Towards Equality*, 283, 8.

44. Hasan, *Politics of Inclusion*, 3.

45. Bhargava, "Democratic Vision of a New Republic," 44.

46. Hasan, *Politics of Inclusion*, 21, 8.

47. Ibid., 19.

48. Chakravarti, *Gendering Caste Through a Feminist Lens*, 140.

CHAPTER 4

1. India, Constituent Assembly, *Debates*, 11:792 (Chaudhuri), 12:1 (Das), 12:2 (Prasad).

2. Varma, *Women's Struggle for Political Space*, 195.

3. Narayan et al., "Enhancing Women's Representation," 5.

4. As of this writing, the bill is still awaiting confirmation by the Lok Sabha.

5. India, Parliament, *Lok Sabha Debates*, series 11, vol. 7, no. 13 (December 9, 1996), 272.

6. See Mohanty, "Panchayat Raj Institutions and Women," for a discussion of the ways in which inclusion in the *panchayat raj* has—and hasn't—contributed to women's active participation in politics.

7. Nanivadekar, "Reservation for Women," 1815.

8. Forbes, *Women in Modern India*, 227.

9. Committee on the Status of Women, *Towards Equality*, 8, 301.

10. Ibid., 302.

11. Ibid., 304, 356.

12. Margaret Alva, interview by Meenakshi Nath, in Nath, "Cutting Across Party Lines," 7.

13. Kishwar, "Out of the Zenana Dabba," 22.

14. Rajan, *Real and Imagined Women*, 116.

15. Visweswaran, *Fictions of Feminist Ethnography*, 98–100.

16. Alva, interview, in Nath, "Cutting Across Party Lines," 7.

17. Pramila Dandavate, interview by Nath, ibid., 13.

18. *Lok Sabha Debates*, series 11, vol. 9, no. 1 (February 25, 1997), 317.

19. Dandavate, interview, in Nath, "Cutting Across Party Lines," 12.

20. In *Recovering Subversion*, Nivedita Menon notes that there were feminist arguments for and against the bill. She explains that although students of the debate tended to cast the bill's detractors as antifeminist, in fact several feminist activists also voiced deep concern about the bill as it was then formulated (171).

21. Uma Bharti, interview by Nath, in Nath, "Cutting Across Party Lines," 9.

22. Dandavate, interview, ibid., 14.

23. Alva, interview, ibid., 9.

24. "Prime Minister Moots Special Facilities, Reservation for Women," *Hindu* (Chennai, India), March 9, 1999.

25. Alva, interview, in Nath, "Cutting Across Party Lines," 10.

26. *Lok Sabha Debates*, series 11, vol. 9, no. 1 (February 25, 1997), 323.

27. "Mulayam Fears an All-Women Parliament," *Times of India* (Mumbai), March 15, 2010.

28. Quoted in "Lalu Wants Rs. 100,000 Pension for MPs," *Times of India* (Mumbai), April 29, 2010.

29. Mitra and Ansari, "Women's Bill: Ladies' Seat," 21.

30. *Lok Sabha Debates*, series 12, vol. 8, no. 9 (March 8, 1999), 6.

31. "Women's Rally in Support of Reservation Bill," *Times of India* (Mumbai), November 23, 2001.

32. Kannabiran and Kannabiran, "From Social Action to Political Action," 197.

33. Gandhi also made this argument, writing, "woman is the embodiment of sacrifice and her advent to public life should . . . result in purifying it." Quoted in Kishwar, "Women and Politics," 2869.

34. Quoted in Sukumar Muralidharan, "A Bill in Vain," PBS *Frontline*, January 10, 1997.

35. Dandavate, interview, in Nath, "Cutting Across Party Lines," 15.

36. Gandhi, "And the One Who Differs," 19.

37. Women politicians often made use of such imagery to great political advantage. For example, in a speech during the 1967 elections, Indira Gandhi told her audience, "Your burdens are relatively light because your families are limited and viable. But my burden is manifold because *crores* of my family members are poverty stricken and I have to look after them." Quoted in Rajan, *Real and Imagined Women*, 110.

38. Quoted in "Mother in Lok Sabha, Papa in Kitchen, If Shabana Has Her Way," Express News Service, March 8, 2002, http://www.expressindia.com/news/fullstory .php?newsid=8162.

39. *Lok Sabha Debates*, series 12, vol. 8, no. 9 (March 8, 1999), 651.

40. Dandavate, interview, in Nath, "Cutting Across Party Lines," 12.

41. Menon, *Recovering Subversion*, 174.

42. Hasan, *Politics of Inclusion*, 8.

43. Ibid., 144.

44. Ibid., 71.

45. Shahabuddin, "Sachar Report."
46. "The Fate of the Bill," *Hindu* (Chennai, India), May 27, 1997.
47. *Lok Sabha Debates,* series 11, vol. 14, no. 8 (May 16, 1997), 468.
48. Ibid., 476.
49. India, Rajya Sabha, *Parliamentary Debates,* No. 219 (March 8, 2010), 17.
50. Menon, *Recovering Subversion,* 174, 180.
51. Alva, interview, in Nath, "Cutting Across Party Lines," 7.
52. Bharti quoted in Menon, *Recovering Subversion,* 174. One of the strengths of the subquota approach to the Women's Reservation Bill is that it would establish a connection between women's and minority group empowerment, forming a congruence between the two at a crucial point. On the one hand, in the bargain underlying the postcolonial social contract, minority men were assured masculinist legal domination in the family but lost measures that would have facilitated minority group political representation. On the other hand, the contract granted women the principle (if not the reality) of political equality but perpetuated their legal subordination within the family. Women belonging to minority communities, of course, lost on both counts; their subordination in the family was countenanced through discriminatory personal laws, and their marginalization in political life resulted in part from the dismantling of measures meant to ensure proportional minority group representation. The quotas-within-quotas approach addresses the fragmentation that produced this outcome.
53. *Lok Sabha Debates,* series 12, vol. 4, no. 21 (July 14, 1998), 269.
54. Ibid., series 13, vol. 5, no. 11 (March 8, 2000), 719.
55. Jenkins, "Competing Inequalities," 54.
56. *Lok Sabha Debates,* series 11, vol. 14, no. 8 (May 16, 1997), 322 (Azmi), 469 (Yadav).
57. "Mulayam Fears an All-Women Parliament," *Times of India* (Mumbai), March 15, 2010.
58. "Furor in Lok Sabha over Women's Quota Bill," *Hindu* (Chennai, India), April 17, 1997.
59. *Lok Sabha Debates,* series 12, vol. 4, no. 21 (July 14, 1998), 248; vol. 7, no. 11 (December 14, 1998), 444.
60. Ibid., series 13, vol. 15, no. 11 (March 8, 2001), 239.
61. The Women's Reservation Bill was introduced on International Women's Day 2010, but Parliament had to be dismissed soon afterward because several members sought to block consideration of the bill by creating chaos on the floor of the House. Although debate resumed the next day, several members had to be evicted from the proceedings. Ultimately, however, the bill passed, with only one MP voting against it.
62. Rajya Sabha, *Parliamentary Debates,* No. 219 (March 9, 2010), 31–32.
63. B. S. Raghavan, "Three Cheers for Women's Reservation Bill!" *Hindu* (Chennai, India), March 8, 2010.
64. Rajya Sabha, *Parliamentary Debates,* No. 219 (March 9, 2010), 32.

CHAPTER 5

1. India, Parliament, *Parliamentary Debates: Official Report,* vol. 15, part 2 (September 20, 1951), 2943.
2. Ibid., *Official Report,* vol. 16, part 2 (October 11, 1951), 4736.
3. For an excellent discussion of the distinction between legal pluralism and legal universalism in various phases of modern Indian politics, see Rudolph and Rudolph, "Living with Difference in India."

4. Explanatory statement prefixed to the draft code submitted by the members in 1944, quoted in Sarkar, "Reform of Hindu Marriage," 102. The two main schools were the Mitakshara and the Dayabhaga, each linked to different areas of the country. In addition, there were many subschools of family law as well as customary laws (100).

5. Forbes, *Women in Modern India*, 118; Sarkar, *Hindu Wife, Hindu Nation*, 102; Agnes, *Law and Gender Inequality*, 198.

6. Choudhury, *Uniform Civil Code*, 39.

7. *Parliamentary Debates: Official Report*, vol. 15, part 2 (September 20, 1951), 2943.

8. Quoted in Sreenath and Sreenath, "Dr. Ambedkar," 299.

9. Choudhury, *Uniform Civil Code*, 40.

10. Derrett, *Religion, Law, and the State in India*, 330.

11. Kishwar, "Codified Hindu Law," 2153.

12. Ibid., 2145.

13. Agnes, *Law and Gender Inequality*, xxxiii.

14. Rudolph and Rudolph, "Living with Difference in India," 33.

15. Despite legislation invalidating them, many of these more gender-just practices continue to be followed.

16. Agnes, *Law and Gender Inequality*, xviii.

17. For more on this point, see Banerjee, *Make Me a Man!*

18. Hasan, "Muslim Women and the Debate on Legal Reforms," 122.

19. Kishwar, "Pro-Women or Anti-Muslim?" 4.

20. Calman, *Toward Empowerment*, 160.

21. Hasan, "Minority Identity," 68, 59.

22. Varshney, "Contested Meanings," 227.

23. Hasan, "Minority Identity," 68, 67.

24. See Hasan's introduction to *Forging Identities*, xvi.

25. Pathak and Rajan, "Shah Bano," 567.

26. Kishwar, "Pro-Women or Anti-Muslim?" 5.

27. Paul Iredale, "Indian Opposition Blasts Congress at Convention," Reuters North American Wire, November 10, 1995.

28. Kishwar, "Pro-Women or Anti-Muslim?" 11. It is a reflection of the entrenchment of fraternalist pluralist politics that when the BJP was in power from 1999 to 2004, it did not attempt to enact such a code. Susanne and Lloyd Rudolph explain that "in its quest to become the dominant party in a diverse multicultural land, the Hindu nationalist BJP . . . has shown movement towards the policies that governments in a multi-cultural society find prudent to embrace, recognizing and valuing difference rather than denigrating or eradicating it." "Living with Difference in India," 35.

29. Agnes, *Law and Gender Inequality*, 205, 193. Agnes explains, however, that although polygamy is outlawed by Hindu law and permitted by Muslim law, "polygamous marriages are in fact as frequent among Hindus (5.8%) as among the Muslims (5.7%)" (193).

30. Merchant, "Divorce Among Indian Muslims," 12.

31. Agnes, *Law and Gender Inequality*, xlii, xlv.

32. Menski, "Indian Secular Pluralism," 35.

33. Ibid., 43.

34. Bano, "Muslim Women's Voices," 2982.

35. Chhachhi, "Identity Politics, Secularism, and Women," 92.

36. In 2005 as well, the AIMPLB set out a divorce code that recommends against the practice of triple *talaq*.

37. Abdi quoted in Sutapa Mukerjee, "India's Muslims Face Up to Rifts," BBC News online, http://news.bbc.co.uk/2/hi/south_asia/4235999.stm.

38. Roy, "Not by Law Alone," 27–28.

39. "Who's Afraid of the Supreme Court?" 45.

40. Menon, "State, Community, and the Debate," 88.

41. Shachar, *Multicultural Jurisdictions*, 146, 2. Shachar further explains that the term "identity groups" "can also apply to other types of minority groups, such as those organized primarily along ethnic, racial, tribal, or national-origin lines, as long as their members share a comprehensive and distinguishable worldview that extends to creating a law for the community. . . . Such groups . . . share a unique history and collective memory, a distinct culture, a set of social norms, customs, and traditions, or perhaps an experience of maltreatment by mainstream society or oppression by the state, all of which may give rise to a set of group specific rules or practices" (2).

42. Ibid., 139.

CONCLUSION

1. Mills, "Contract of Breach: Repairing the Racial Contract," in Pateman and Mills, *Contract and Domination*, 110.

2. Pateman, "Contract and Social Change: A Dialogue Between Carole Pateman and Charles Mills," in ibid., 15.

3. Ibid.

4. See Lorde, "Master's Tools," 110.

5. Brown, *States of Injury*, 138.

6. Ibid.

7. Sangtin Collective and Richa Nagar, *Playing with Fire*, 12.

8. For an excellent discussion of the political efficacy, as well as the ethical and philosophical coherence, of linking together seemingly disparate approaches to social transformation, see Sandoval, *Methodology of the Oppressed*.

9. See http://www.unmarried.org/statistics.html. The figure of 11 million includes 1.2 million people cohabiting with same-sex partners; their decision to live together rather than marry cannot be considered a choice, however, given the restrictions on same-sex marriage in the vast majority of U.S. states.

10. For an insightful short treatment of marriage and what more needs to be done to transform the marriage contract, see Shanley, Cohen, and Chasman, *Just Marriage*.

11. In *Contract and Domination*, Charles Mills translates this insight into the language and framework of social contract theory and uses the term "subcontractors" for those who cannot be full partners in the exclusionary social contract (which he calls the "racia-sexual contract," linking together the racial and the sexual contracts) but can participate in and benefit from aspects of it. Unlike women of color in the United States, who can be considered noncontractors in the sense that the "racia-sexual contract" secures their exploitation and domination in terms of both race and gender, white women secure racial power and privilege and men of color secure gender power and privilege from the contract. One of the effects of this positioning in building social movements against racial and gender oppression is that subcontractors are likely to challenge only those aspects of the contract that subordinate them in particular, because "the racia-sexual contract offers the option, which will be both ideologically dominant and politically most appealing, of a partitioned struggle against one aspect of the contract that meanwhile maintains the other." Subcontracting thus "will always seem more attractive than fighting for the tearing up of the contract altogether" (188). The challenge here is how to motivate those who hold intragroup power and privilege to tear up the contract.

12. See http://www.incite-national.org/ for an overview of Incite! and its work, and http://harmfreezone.org/hfz-booklet.pdf and http://www.southerncoalition.org/ harmfree for descriptions of harm-free zones.

13. Shapiro, *State of Democratic Theory*, 3.

14. See Watkins, "Conceptualizing Democracy in a Global Era," 99–119.

15. Pettit, *Republicanism*, 164.

16. Watkins, "Conceptualizing Democracy in a Global Era," 99–119.

17. Shapiro, *State of Democratic Theory*, 4.

18. Pettit, *Republicanism*, 164.

19. Shapiro, *State of Democratic Theory*, 18.

20. Cornell, *At the Heart of Freedom*, 174, 185, 186.

21. This mode of hopefulness can be contrasted with other forms of hope. Indeed, like much else in democratic theory, hope is a contested concept even among those who advocate it, especially in relation to the questions of what we should hope for and to whom we should direct our hopes. In *National Manhood*, for example, Dana Nelson critiques "presidentialism" as a mode of hopefulness in the United States. By presidentialism she means the "constitutionally conditioned habit of looking to the President" instead of to one another for societal change. She argues that presidentialism forecloses or short-circuits our democratic impulses and energies, such that "alternative possibilities and practices (and even our ability to imagine those possibilities) get blocked" (205). One of the features that make presidentialism so compelling, according to Nelson, is that even as we disparage or despise a current president, we hope that someone better, someone more deserving of our trust and loyalty, is on the horizon. In Nelson's view, the centrality of discourses of hope in so much U.S. election rhetoric is not surprising. She argues that challenging presidentialism involves refocusing our attention on one another and engaging in what she calls "the difficult, ongoing process of creating and recreating equalitarian grounds for reciprocally dissensual democratic processes" (223).

22. Gandhi, *Hind Swaraj and Other Writings*, 39.

BIBLIOGRAPHY

Agnes, Flavia. *Law and Gender Inequality: The Politics of Women's Rights in India.* New Delhi: Oxford University Press, 1999.

Alexander, M. Jacqui, and Chandra Talpade Mohanty, eds. *Feminist Genealogies, Colonial Legacies, Democratic Futures.* New York: Routledge, 1997.

Ali, Azra Asghar. *The Emergence of Feminism Among Indian Muslim Women, 1920–1947.* Oxford: Oxford University Press, 2000.

Allen, Paula Gunn. *The Sacred Hoop: Recovering the Feminine in American Indian Traditions.* Boston: Beacon Press, 1992.

Alvarez, Sonia E., Evelina Dagnino, and Arturo Escobar. *Cultures of Politics/Politics of Cultures: Revisioning Latin American Social Movements.* Boulder, Colo.: Westview Press, 1998.

Appadurai, Arjun. *Modernity at Large: Cultural Dimensions of Globalization.* Minneapolis: University of Minnesota Press, 1996.

Austin, Granville. *The Indian Constitution: Cornerstone of a Nation.* London: Oxford University Press, 1966.

———. *Working a Democratic Constitution: The Indian Experience.* New Delhi: Oxford University Press, 2000.

Baber, Zaheer. "'Race,' Religion, and Riots: The Racialization of Communal Identity and Conflict in India." *Sociology* 38, no. 4 (2004): 701–18.

Bajpai, Rochana. "Constituent Assembly Debates and Minority Rights." *Economic and Political Weekly* 35 (May 27, 1990): 1837–45.

Ballantyne, Tony. *Orientalism and Race: Aryanism in the British Empire.* New York: Palgrave, 2002.

Banerjee, Sikata. *Make Me a Man! Masculinity, Hinduism, and Nationality in India.* Albany: SUNY Press, 2005.

Bano, Sabeeha. "Muslim Women's Voices: Expanding Gender Justice Under Muslim Law." *Economic and Political Weekly* 30 (November 25, 1995): 2981–82.

Barber, Benjamin. *Strong Democracy: Participatory Politics for a New Age.* Berkeley and Los Angeles: University of California Press, 1984.

Barnett, Marguerite Ross. *The Politics of Cultural Nationalism in South India.* Princeton: Princeton University Press, 1976.

Basu, Aparna, and Bharati Ray, eds. *From Independence Toward Freedom: Essays on Indian Women Since 1947.* New Delhi: Oxford University Press, 1999.

———. *Women's Struggle: A History of the All-India Women's Conference, 1927–2002.* New Delhi: Manohar, 2003.

Basu, Srimati. *She Comes to Take Her Rights: Indian Women, Property, and Propriety.* Albany: SUNY Press, 1999.

Baxamusa, Ramala. *The Legal Status of Muslim Women: An Appraisal of Muslim Personal Law in India.* Mumbai: Research Centre for Women's Studies, 1998.

Benhabib, Seyla. *Claims of Culture: Equality and Diversity in the Global Era.* Princeton: Princeton University Press, 2002.

Bhargava, Rajeev. "Democratic Vision of a New Republic: India, 1950." In *Transforming India: Social and Political Dynamics of Democracy,* ed. Francine R. Frankel, Zoya Hasan, Rajeev Bhargava, and Balveer Arora, 26–59. New York: Oxford University Press, 2002.

———. *Secularism and Its Critics.* New Delhi: Oxford University Press, 1998.

Brass, Paul. *The Politics of India Since Independence.* Cambridge: Cambridge University Press, 1994.

———. "The Strong State and the Fear of Disorder." In *Transforming India: Social and Political Dynamics of Democracy,* ed. Francine R. Frankel, Zoya Hasan, Rajeev Bhargava, and Balveer Arora, 60–88. New York: Oxford University Press, 2002.

Brown, Elsa Barkley. "'What Has Happened Here?': The Politics of Difference in Women's History and Feminist Politics." *Feminist Studies* 18 (Summer 1992): 295–312.

Brown, Wendy. *States of Injury.* Princeton: Princeton University Press, 1995.

Butler, Judith, and Joan W. Scott, eds. *Feminists Theorize the Political.* New York: Routledge, 1992.

Calman, Leslie. *Toward Empowerment: Women and Movement Politics in India.* Boulder, Colo.: Westview Press, 1992.

Cannon, Garland Hapton. *The Life and Mind of Oriental Jones: Sir William Jones, the Father of Modern Linguistics.* Cambridge: Cambridge University Press, 1991.

Chakravarti, Uma. *Gendering Caste Through a Feminist Lens.* New Delhi: Stree, 2003.

———. "Whatever Happened to the Vedic Dasi? Orientalism, Nationalism, and a Script for the Past." In *Recasting Women: Essays in Colonial History,* ed. Kumkum Sangari and Sudesh Vaid, 27–87. New Delhi: Kali for Women, 1989.

Chatterjee, Partha. "Beyond the Nation? Or Within?" *Economic and Political Weekly* 32 (January 4–11, 1997): 30–34.

———. *The Nation and Its Fragments: Colonial and Postcolonial Histories.* Princeton: Princeton University Press, 1993.

Chattopadhyaya, Kamaladevi. *The Awakening of Indian Women.* Madras: Everyman's Press, 1939.

———. "Oral History." Oral History Interview Transcript. New Delhi: Nehru Memorial Museum and Library, 1980.

Chhachhi, Amrita. "Identity Politics, Secularism, and Women." In *Forging Identities: Gender, Communities, and the State,* ed. Zoya Hasan, 74–95. New Delhi: Kali for Women, 1994.

Choudhury, Arundhati Roy. *Uniform Civil Code: Social Change and Gender Justice.* New Delhi: Indian Social Institute, 1998.

Cohen, Joshua, and Joel Rogers. *On Democracy.* Middlesex, UK: Penguin Books, 1983.

Cornell, Drucilla. *At the Heart of Freedom: Feminism, Sex, and Equality.* Princeton: Princeton University Press, 1998.

Cousins, Margaret. *Indian Womanhood Today.* Allahabad: Kitabistan Press, 1941.

———. "What Women Have Gained by the Reform." In Muthulakshmi Reddi, *Speeches and Writings*, vol. 1, 97–98. S. Muthulakshmi Reddi Papers, Nehru Memorial Museum and Library, New Delhi.

Crenshaw, Kimberlé. "Mapping the Margins: Intersectionality, Identity Politics, and Violence Against Women of Color." In *Critical Race Theory*, ed. Kimberlé Crenshaw, Neil Gotanda, Garry Peller, and Kendall Thomas, 357–83. New York: New Press, 1995.

Dallmayr, Fred. "Beyond Monologue: For a Comparative Political Theory." *Perspectives on Politics* 2, no. 2 (2004): 249–57.

———. *Border Crossings: Towards a Comparative Political Theory.* Lanham, Md.: Lexington Books, 1999.

Derrett, J. Duncan. *Religion, Law, and the State in India.* New York: Free Press, 1968.

Desai, A. R., ed. *Women's Liberation and Politics of Religious Personal Laws in India.* Bombay: C. G. Shah Memorial Trust, 1990.

De Sousa Santos, Boaventura. *Democratizing Democracy: Beyond the Liberal Democratic Canon.* London: Verso, 2006.

Devendra, Kiran. *Status and Position of Women in India.* New Delhi: Shakti Books, 1986.

Devi, Mahasweta. *Imaginary Maps.* Translated by Gayatri Chakravorty Spivak. Calcutta: Thema, 1993.

Dirks, Nicholas. *Castes of Mind: Colonialism and the Making of Modern India.* Princeton: Princeton University Press, 2001.

Engineer, Ashgar Ali. *The Rights of Women in Islam.* London: C. Hurst, 1992.

Enloe, Cynthia. *Bananas, Beaches, and Bases.* Berkeley and Los Angeles: University of California Press, 1989.

———. *The Morning After.* Berkeley and Los Angeles: University of California Press, 1993.

Flax, Jane. *The American Dream in Black and White: The Clarence Thomas Hearings.* Ithaca: Cornell University Press, 1998.

Fletcher, Ian Christopher, Laura E. Nym Mayhall, and Phillipa Levine, eds. *Women's Suffrage in the British Empire: Citizenship, Nation, and Race.* London: Routledge, 2000.

Forbes, Geraldine. *Women in Modern India.* Cambridge: Cambridge University Press, 1996.

Foucault, Michel. "Nietzsche, Genealogy, History." In *Language, Counter-Memory, Practice.* Translated by Donald L. Bouchard and Sherry Simon. Ithaca: Cornell University Press, 1977.

Frankel, Francine R., Zoya Hasan, Rajeev Bhargava, and Balveer Arora, eds. *Transforming India: Social and Political Dynamics of Democracy.* New York: Oxford University Press, 2002.

Fraser, Nancy. "Beyond the Master/Subject Model: Reflections on Pateman's *The Sexual Contract.*" *Social Text* 37 (Winter 1993): 173–81.

Galanter, Marc. *Law and Society in Modern India.* New Delhi: Oxford University Press, 1989.

Gandhi, Mahatma. *All Men Are Brothers: Life and Thoughts of Mahatma Gandhi as Told in His Own Words.* Compiled and edited by Krishna Kripalani. New York: Columbia University Press and UNESCO, 1958.

———. *Hind Swaraj and Other Writings.* Edited by Anthony Parel. Cambridge: Cambridge University Press, 1997.

Gandhi, Maneka. "And the One Who Differs . . . Maneka Gandhi on Women in Politics." *Manushi* 96 (September–October 1996): 15.

Gellner, Ernest. *Nations and Nationalism*. Ithaca: Cornell University Press, 1983.

Gibson-Graham, J. K. *The End of Capitalism (as We Knew It): A Feminist Critique of Political Economy*. Oxford: Blackwell, 1996.

Grant, Charles. "Observations on the State of Society Among the Asiatic Subjects of Great Britain, Particularly with Respect of Morals, and on the Means of Improving It." 1796. Parliamentary Papers 10, no. 282. London: House of Commons, 1813.

Guha, Ramachandra. *India After Gandhi: The History of the World's Largest Democracy*. London: Macmillan, 2007.

Hardgrave, Robert. *Essays in the Political Sociology of South India*. New Delhi: USHA Publications, 1979.

Harvey, David. *The Condition of Postmodernity*. Cambridge, Mass.: Blackwell, 1990.

Hasan, Zoya. "Minority Identity, State Policy, and Political Process." In *Forging Identities: Gender, Communities, and the State*, ed. Zoya Hasan, 59–74. New Delhi: Kali for Women, 1994.

———. "Muslim Women and the Debate on Legal Reforms." In *From Independence Toward Freedom: Essays on Indian Women Since 1947*, ed. Aparna Basu and Bharati Ray, 120–34. New Delhi: Oxford University Press, 1999.

———. *Politics of Inclusion: Castes, Minorities, and Affirmative Action*. New Delhi: Oxford University Press, 2009.

Hasan, Zoya, E. Sridharan, and R. Sudarshan, eds. *India's Living Constitution*. London: Anthem Press, 2005.

Hastings, Warren. "Plan for the Administration of Justice Extracted from the Proceedings of the Committee of Circuit, 15 August 1772." In *Historical Documents of British India*, ed. G. W. Forrest, vol. 2, *Warren Hastings*, 112–15. New Delhi: Anmol Publications, 1985.

Hobbes, Thomas. *The Leviathan*. 1651. Edited by Richard Tuck. Cambridge: Cambridge University Press, 1996.

India. Committee on the Status of Women in India. *Towards Equality: Report of the Committee on the Status of Women in India*. New Delhi: Indian Ministry of Education and Social Welfare, Department of Social Welfare, 1974.

India. Constituent Assembly. *Debates: Official Report* [legislative], 1st sess., vols. 2–3. New Delhi: Manager of Publications, 1949.

———. *Debates: Official Report*, vols. 1–12. New Delhi: Manager of Publications, 1966.

India. Franchise Committee. *Indian Constitutional Reforms: Reports of the Franchise Committee and the Committee on the Division of Functions*. New Delhi: Superintendent of Government Printing, India, 1919.

India. Parliament. *Parliamentary Debates: Official Report*, vol. 15, part 2 (September 20). New Delhi: Manager of Publications, 1951.

———. *Parliamentary Debates: Official Report*, vol. 16, part 2 (October 11). New Delhi: Manager of Publications, 1951.

India. Parliament. Lok Sabha. *Lok Sabha Debates*. Series 11. New Delhi: Lok Sabha Secretariat, 1996–97.

———. *Lok Sabha Debates*. Series 12. New Delhi: Lok Sabha Secretariat, 1998–99.

———. *Lok Sabha Debates*. Series 13. New Delhi: Lok Sabha Secretariat, 2000–2001.

India. Parliament. Rajya Sabha. *Parliamentary Debates: Official Report, Council of States*. No. 219. New Delhi: Council of States Secretariat, 2010.

India. Parliament Secretariat. *Reports of Committees of the Constituent Assembly of India*. New Delhi: Government of India Press, 1950.

India. Prime Minister's High Level Committee. *Social, Economic, and Educational Status of the Muslim Community in India: A Report*. November 2006. http://minorityaffairs.gov.in/newsite/sachar/sachar_comm.pdf.

Indian Annual Register: An Annual Digest of Public Affairs of India Regarding the Nation's Activities Each Year in Matters Political, Economic, Industrial, Educational, Social, Etc. Calcutta: Annual Register Office, 1931.

Irschick, Eugene. *Politics and Social Conflict in South India*. Berkeley and Los Angeles: University of California Press, 1969.

Jahan, Rounaq. "Women in South Asian Politics." *Third World Quarterly* 9 (July 1987): 848–70.

Jayawardena, Kumari. *Feminism and Nationalism in the Third World*. London: Zed Books, 1986.

———. *The White Woman's Other Burden: Western Women and South Asia During British Rule*. New York: Routledge, 1995.

Jenkins, Laura Dudley. "Competing Inequalities: The Struggle over Reserved Seats for Women in India." *International Review of Social History* 44 (1999): 53–75.

Jones, William. *The Letters of Sir William Jones*. Edited by Garland Hapton Cannon. London: Oxford University Press, 1970.

Jung, Hwa Hol, ed. *Comparative Political Culture in the Age of Globalization: An Introductory Anthology*. Lanham, Md.: Lexington Books, 2002.

Kandiyoti, Deniz. "Bargaining with Patriarchy." *Gender and Society* 2 (September 1988): 274–90.

Kannabiran, Vasanth, and Kalpana Kannabiran. "From Social Action to Political Action: Women and the Eighty-First Amendment." *Economic and Political Weekly* 32 (February 1, 1997): 196–97.

Kaplan, Caren, Norma Alarcón, and Minoo Moallem, eds. *Between Women and Nation*. Durham: Duke University Press, 1999.

Kapur, Ratna, and Brenda Cossman. "On Women, Equality, and the Constitution: Through the Looking Glass of Feminism." In *Gender and Politics in India*, ed. Nivedita Menon, 197–201. New Delhi: Oxford University Press, 1999.

Kaushik, Susheela. "Women and Political Participation." In *Women in Politics: Forms and Processes*, ed. Kamala Sankaran, 35–54. New Delhi: Friedrich Ebert Stiftung, 1992.

Kazi, Seema. *Muslim Women in India*. London: Minority Rights Group International, 1999.

Kelley, Robin D. G. *Race Rebels*. New York: Free Press, 1994.

Kishwar, Madhu. "Breaking the Stalemate: Uniform Civil Code vs. Personal Law." *Manushi* 77 (July–August 1993): 2–5.

———. "Codified Hindu Law: Myth and Reality." *Economic and Political Weekly* 29 (August 13, 1994): 2145–61.

———. "Gandhi on Women." *Economic and Political Weekly* 20 (October 5, 1985): 1691–1702.

———. "Out of the Zenana Dabba: Strategies for Enhancing Women's Political Representation." *Manushi* 96 (September–October 1996): 21–30.

———. "Pro-Women or Anti-Muslim? The Shah Bano Controversy." *Manushi* 32 (January–February 1986): 4–13.

———. "Women and Politics: Beyond Quotas." *Economic and Political Weekly* 31 (October 26, 1996): 2867–74.

Kumar, Radha. *A History of Doing.* New Delhi: Kali for Women, 1993.

LaClau, Ernesto, and Chantal Mouffe. *Hegemony and Socialist Strategy: Towards a Radical Democratic Politics.* London: Verso Press, 1987.

Lakshmi, C. S. "Mother, Mother Community, and Mother Politics in Tamil Nadu." *Economic and Political Weekly* 25 (October 20–29, 1990): 72–83.

Lessnoff, Michael. *Social Contract.* Atlantic Highlands, N.J.: Humanities Press International, 1986.

Little, Joanna, and Rama Joshi. *Daughters of Independence: Gender, Caste, and Class in India.* New Delhi: Kali for Women, 1986.

Locke, John. *The Second Treatise of Government.* 1689. Edited by C. B. Macpherson. Indianapolis: Hackett, 1980.

Lorde, Audre. "The Master's Tools Will Never Dismantle the Master's House." In Lorde, *Sister Outsider: Essays and Speeches,* 110–13. Berkeley: Crossing Press, 1984.

Lugones, María. "Heterosexualism and the Colonial/Modern Gender System." *Hypatia* 22 (Winter 2007): 186–209.

———. *Pilgrimages, Peregrinajes: Theorizing Coalition Against Multiple Oppressions.* Lanham, Md.: Rowman and Littlefield, 2003.

Macpherson, C. B. *The Life and Times of Liberal Democracy.* London: Oxford University Press, 1977.

Mahan, Rajan. *Women in Indian National Congress.* New Delhi: Rawat Publications, 1999.

Mani, Lata. *Contentious Traditions: The Debate on Sati in Colonial India.* Berkeley and Los Angeles: University of California Press, 1998.

McClintock, Anne, Aamir Mufti, and Ella Shohat, eds. *Dangerous Liaisons: Gender, Nation, and Postcolonial Perspectives.* Minneapolis: University of Minnesota Press, 1997.

Mehta, Uday Singh. *Liberalism and Empire.* Chicago: University of Chicago Press, 1999.

Menon, Nivedita. *Gender and Politics in India.* New Delhi: Oxford University Press, 1999.

———. *Recovering Subversion: Feminist Politics Beyond the Law.* Urbana: University of Illinois Press, 2004.

———. "State, Community, and the Debate on the Uniform Civil Code in India." In *Beyond Rights Talk and Culture Talk: Comparative Essays on the Politics and Rights of Culture,* ed. Mahmood Mamdani, 75–96. New York: St. Martin's Press, 2000.

Menski, Werner. "Indian Secular Pluralism and Its Relevance for Europe." In *Legal Practice and Cultural Diversity,* ed. Ralph Grillo, Roger Ballard, Alessandro Ferrari, Andras J. Hoekema, Marcel Maussen, Prakash Shah, Deborah Parry, Annette Nordhausen and Geraint Howells, 31–48. London: Ashgate Press, 2009.

Merchant, Munira. "Divorce Among Indian Muslims: Survey Report from Bombay and Pune." *Manushi* 77 (July–August 1993): 12–13.

Mies, Maria. *Patriarchy and Accumulation on a World Scale: Women in the International Division of Labour.* London: Zed Books, 1998.

Mill, James. *The History of British India.* 1817. New Delhi: Associated Publishing House, 1990.

Mills, Charles. "Race and the Social Contract Tradition." Paper delivered at the annual meeting of the American Political Science Association, Atlanta, Georgia, September 2–5, 1999.

———. *The Racial Contract.* Ithaca: Cornell University Press, 1997.

Misra, Panchanand. *The Making of the Indian Republic: Some Aspects of India's Constitution in the Making.* Calcutta: Scientific Book Agency, 1966.

Mitra, Sumit, and Javed Ansari. "Women's Bill: Ladies' Seat." *India Today,* July 16, 1998, 21.

Mohanty, Bidyut. "Panchayat Raj Institutions and Women." In *From Independence Toward Freedom: Essays on Indian Women Since 1947,* ed. Aparna Basu and Bharati Ray, 19–33. New Delhi: Oxford University Press, 1999.

Montagu, Edwin. *An Indian Diary.* London: William Heinemann, 1930.

Muthu, Sankar. *Enlightenment Against Empire.* Princeton: Princeton University Press, 2003.

Nandy, Ashis. *At the Edge of Psychology: Essays in Politics and Culture.* New Delhi: Oxford University Press, 1980.

Nanivadekar, Medha. "Reservation for Women: Challenge of Tackling Counter-Productive Trends." *Economic and Political Weekly* 33 (July 11, 1998): 1815–18.

Narayan, Jayaprakash, Dhirubhai Sheth, Yogendra Yadav, and Madhu Kishwar. "Enhancing Women's Representation in Legislatures: An Alternative to the Government Bill for Women's Reservation." *Manushi* 116 (January–February 2000): 5–12. http://www.indiatogether.org/manushi/issue116/alterbill.htm.

Nath, Meenakshi. "Cutting Across Party Lines: Women Members of Parliament Explain Their Stand on Reservation Quotas." *Manushi* 96 (September–October 1996): 7–16.

Nelson, Dana. *National Manhood: Capitalist Citizenship and the Imagined Fraternity of White Men.* Durham: Duke University Press, 1998.

Okin, Susan Moller. *Is Multiculturalism Good for Women?* Princeton: Princeton University Press, 1999.

Olson, Joel. *The Abolition of White Democracy.* Minneapolis: University of Minnesota Press, 2004.

Omvedt, Gail. "Women, Zilla Parishads, and Panchayat Raj: Chandwad to Vitner." *Economic and Political Weekly* 25 (August 4, 1990): 1687–90.

Oyewumi, Oyeronke. *The Invention of Women: Making African Sense Out of Western Gender Discourses.* Minneapolis: University of Minnesota Press, 1997.

Pandey, Gyanendra. *The Construction of Communalism in Colonial North India.* New York: Oxford University Press, 1990.

Pandian, Jacob. *Caste, Nationalism, and Ethnicity: An Interpretation of Tamil Cultural History and Social Order.* Bombay: Popular Prakashan, 1987.

Parashar, Archana. *Women and Family Law Reform in India.* New Delhi: Sage Publications, 1992.

Parel, Anthony. "The Comparative Study of Political Philosophy." In *Comparative Political Philosophy: Studies Under the Upas Tree,* ed. Anthony Parel and Ronald Keith, 11–29. New Delhi: Sage Publications, 1992.

Patankar, Bharat, and Gail Omvedt. "The Dalit Liberation Movement in the Colonial Period." *Economic and Political Weekly* 14 (February 1979): 409–24.

Pateman, Carole. *The Disorder of Women: Democracy, Feminism, and Political Theory.* Stanford: Stanford University Press, 1989.

———. *Participation and Democratic Theory.* Cambridge: Cambridge University Press, 1970.

———. *The Problem of Political Obligation: A Critical Analysis of Liberal Theory.* Berkeley and Los Angeles: University of California Press, 1985.

———. *The Sexual Contract.* Cambridge: Polity Press, 1988.

Pateman, Carole, and Charles Mills. *Contract and Domination.* Cambridge: Polity Press, 2007.

Pathak, Zakia, and Rajeswari Sunder Rajan. "Shah Bano." *Signs* 14 (Spring 1989): 567–89.

Patkar, Medha. "The Struggle for Participation and Justice: A Historical Narrative." In *Towards Sustainable Development? Struggling over Narmada's River,* ed. William Fisher, 159–78. Jaipur: Rawat Publications, 1997.

Pettit, Phillip. *Republicanism: A Theory of Freedom and Government.* Oxford: Oxford University Press, 1997.

Phillips, Anne. *Engendering Democracy.* University Park: Pennsylvania State University Press, 1991.

Pitts, Jennifer. *A Turn to Empire: The Rise of Imperial Liberalism in Britain and France.* Princeton: Princeton University Press, 2006.

Quijano, Anibal. "Coloniality of Power and Eurocentrism in Latin America." *International Sociology* 15, no. 2 (2000): 215–32.

Radhakrishnan, R. "Nationalism, Gender, and the Narrative of Identity." In *Nationalisms and Sexualities,* ed. Andrew Parker, Mary Russo, Dorris Sommer, and Patricia Yaeger, 77–95. New York: Routledge, 1992.

Rajan, Rajeswari Sunder. *Real and Imagined Women: Gender, Culture, and Postcolonialism.* London: Routledge, 1993.

———. *The Scandal of the State: Women, Law, and Citizenship in Postcolonial India.* Durham: Duke University Press, 2003.

Ramasami, E. V. "The Genesis of My Self-Respect Movement." In *Collected Works of Thanthai Periyar E. V. Ramasami.* Madras: Periyar Self-Respect Propaganda Institution, 1981.

Rao, B. Shiva. *The Framing of India's Constitution.* New Delhi: Indian Institute of Public Administration, 1968.

Rau, B. N. *India's Constitution in the Making.* Bombay: Orient Longmans, 1960.

Rawls, John. *A Theory of Justice.* Cambridge: Harvard University Press, 1971.

Ray, Renuka. "Oral History." Oral History Interview Transcript, 1980. Nehru Memorial Museum and Library, New Delhi.

Reddi, Muthulakshmi. *Speeches and Writings.* Vols. 1–2. S. Muthulakshmi Reddi Papers, Nehru Memorial Museum and Library, New Delhi.

Rocher, Rosanne. "British Orientalism in the Eighteenth Century: The Dialectics of Knowledge and Government." In *Orientalism and the Postcolonial Predicament: Perspectives on South Asia,* ed. Peter van de Veer and Carol Breckenridge, 215–49. Philadelphia: University of Pennsylvania Press, 1993.

Rousseau, Jean-Jacques. "Discourse on the Origin of Inequality Among Men." 1755. In *The Basic Political Writings,* trans. Donald A. Cress, 25–82. Indianapolis: Hackett, 1987.

Roy, Mary. "Not by Law Alone." *Manushi* 37 (November–December 1986): 27–28.

Rudolph, Susanne Hoeber, and Lloyd I. Rudolph. "Living with Difference in India." *Political Quarterly* 71 (2000): 20–38.

Sandoval, Chela. *Methodology of the Oppressed.* Minneapolis: University of Minnesota Press, 2000.

Sangari, Kumkum, and Sudesh Vaid. "Recasting Women: An Introduction." In *Recasting Women: Essays in Colonial History,* ed. Kumkum Sangari and Sudesh Vaid, 1–27. New Delhi: Kali for Women, 1989.

Sangtin Collective and Richa Nagar. *Playing with Fire: Feminist Thought and Activism Through Seven Lives in India.* Minneapolis: University of Minnesota Press, 2006.

Sarkar, Lotika. "Reform of Hindu Marriage and Succession Laws: Still the Unequal Sex." In *From Independence Toward Freedom: Essays on Indian Women Since 1947,* ed. Aparna Basu and Bharati Ray, 100–119. New Delhi: Oxford University Press, 1999.

Sarkar, Sumit. *Modern India, 1885–1947.* London: Macmillan, 1989.

Sarkar, Tanika. *Hindu Wife, Hindu Nation: Community, Religion, and Cultural Nationalism.* Bloomington: Indiana University Press, 2001.

Sathe, S. P. *Towards Gender Justice.* Bombay: Research Centre for Women's Studies, 1993.

Scott, James. *Domination and the Arts of Resistance.* New Haven: Yale University Press, 1990.

Shachar, Ayelet. *Multicultural Jurisdictions: Cultural Differences and Women's Rights.* Cambridge: Cambridge University Press, 2001.

Shahabuddin, Syed. "Sachar Report: Flawed Report on Muslims." *Milli Gazette,* January 15, 2007. http://www.milligazette.com/dailyupdate/2007/20070111_Sachar_Report_Flawed_Muslims.htm.

Shams, Shamsuddin, ed. *Women, Law, and Social Change.* New Delhi: Ashish, 1991.

Shanley, Mary Lyndon, Joshua Cohen, and Deborah Chasman, eds. *Just Marriage.* Oxford: Oxford University Press, 2004.

Shapiro, Ian. *The State of Democratic Theory.* Princeton: Princeton University Press, 2003.

Sharpe, Jenny. *Allegories of Empire: The Figure of Woman in the Colonial Text.* Minneapolis: University of Minnesota Press, 1993.

Shohat, Ella, and Robert Stam. *Unthinking Eurocentrism: Multiculturalism and the Media.* London: Routledge, 1994.

Singh, Kirti. "Women's Rights and the Reform of Personal Laws." In *Hindus and Others: The Question of Identity in India Today,* ed. Gyanendra Pandey, 177–96. New Delhi: Penguin Books, 1993.

Sinha, Mrinalini. *Colonial Masculinity: The "Manly Englishman" and the "Effeminate Bengali."* Manchester: Manchester University Press, 1995.

———. *Specters of Mother India.* Durham: Duke University Press, 2006.

Smith, Andrea. *Conquest.* Cambridge, Mass.: South End Press, 2005.

Spivak, Gayatri Chakravorty. "Can the Subaltern Speak?" In *Marxism and the Interpretation of Culture,* ed. Cary Nelson and Lawrence Grossberg, 271–313. Urbana: University of Illinois Press, 1988.

———. "Criticism, Feminism, and the Institution." In *The Postcolonial Critic: Interviews, Strategies, and Dialogues,* ed. Sarah Harasym, 175–89. New York: Routledge, 1990.

————. *In Other Worlds: Essays in Cultural Politics*. London: Routledge, 1988.

————. *Thinking Academic Freedom in Gendered Post-Coloniality*. Capetown: University of Capetown Press, 1992.

————. "Women in Difference: Mahasweta Devi's 'Douloti the Beautiful.'" In *Nationalisms and Sexualities*, ed. Andrew Parker, Mary Russo, Dorris Sommer, and Patricia Yaeger, 96–117. New York: Routledge, 1992.

Sreenath, Lalitha, and M. R. Sreenath. "Dr. Ambedkar, Women, and the Weaker Sections of Society." In *B. R. Ambedkar: Study in Law and Society*, ed. Mohammad Shabbir, 297–317. New Delhi: Rawat Publications, 1997.

Stein, Burton. *A History of India*. Oxford: Blackwell, 1998.

Stoler, Anne. "Carnal Knowledge and Imperial Power: Gender, Race, and Morality in Colonial Asia." In *Gender at the Crossroads of Knowledge: Feminist Anthropology in a Postmodern Era*, ed. Micaela di Leonardo, 51–101. Berkeley and Los Angeles: University of California Press, 1991.

Thapar, Romila. "Interpretations of Indian History: Colonial, Nationalist, Postcolonial." In *Contemporary India: Transitions*, ed. Peter Ronald deSouza, 11–22. New Delhi: Sage Publications, 2000.

Thomas, Megan. "Orientalism and Comparative Political Theory." *Review of Politics* 72, no. 4 (2010): 653–77.

Trautmann, Thomas R. *Aryans and British India*. Berkeley and Los Angeles: University of California Press, 1997.

Varma, Sudhir. *Women's Struggle for Political Space: From Enfranchisement to Participation*. New Delhi: Rawat Publications, 1997.

Varshney, Ashutosh. "Contested Meanings: India's National Identity, Hindu Nationalism, and the Politics of Anxiety." *Daedalus* 122 (June 22, 1993): 227–61.

Vatuk, Sylvia. "Islamic Feminism in India: Indian Muslim Women Activists and the Reform of Muslim Personal Law." *Modern Asian Studies* 42, nos. 2–3 (2008): 489–518.

Visweswaran, Kamala. *Fictions of Feminist Ethnography*. Minneapolis: University of Minnesota Press, 1994.

Watkins, David. "Conceptualizing Democracy in a Global Era." PhD diss., University of Washington, 2008.

"Who's Afraid of the Supreme Court? Follow-Up on the Mary Roy Case." *Manushi* 42–43 (September–December 1987): 45–46.

Wilford, Rick, and Robert Miller, eds. *Women, Ethnicity, and Nationalism: The Politics of Transition*. London: Routledge, 1998.

Williams, Brackette F., ed. *Women Out of Place: The Gender of Agency and the Race of Nationality*. New York: Routledge, 1996.

Winant, Howard. *The World Is a Ghetto: Race and Democracy Since World War II*. New York: Basic Books, 2001.

Young, Crawford. *The Rising Tide of Cultural Pluralism*. Madison: University of Wisconsin Press, 1993.

Young, Robert. *Postcolonialism: An Historical Introduction*. Oxford: Blackwell, 2001.

Yuval-Davis, Nira. "Gender and Nation." *Ethnic and Racial Studies* 16 (October 1993): 621–31.

————. *Gender and Nation*. London: Sage Publications, 1997.

Zaidi, Askari. "Resistance from Within: Muslims Against the Practice of Triple Divorce." *Manushi* 77 (July–August 1993): 6–8.

INDEX

CPSIA information can be obtained at www.ICGtesting.com
Printed in the USA
BVOW07s1954060114

341049BV00002B/80/P